A Call to Russia

A Call to Russia

Glimpses of Missionary Life

From the Journal of a Mission President in the
Russia St. Petersburg Mission

Thomas F. Rogers

Afterword by Gary Anderson

BYU Studies
Brigham Young University
Provo, Utah

BYU Studies Monographs

ISBN 0-8425-2461-4

Printed in the United States of America
10 9 8 7 6 5 4 3 2 1

To the memory of

Sister Marina Abramova, Russia St. Petersburg Mission
President Richard Chapple, Russia Moscow Mission
Elder Douglas Dewey, Russia Moscow Mission
Dr. Richard Huish, Russia Moscow and Ekaterinburg Missions
President Dale Warner, Russia and Bulgaria Missions
President Cordell Wold, Russia Samara Mission

who gave their last full measure
for the kingdom

And thus we see how great the inequality of man is because of sin and transgression, and the power of the devil, which comes by the cunning plans which he hath devised to ensnare the hearts of men.

And thus we see the great call of diligence of men to labor in the vineyards of the Lord; and thus we see the great reason of sorrow, and also of rejoicing—sorrow because of death and destruction among men, and joy because of the light of Christ unto life.

—Alma 28:13–14

Table of Contents

Preface

The decision to publish portions of my journal came about through a series of seemingly random events. While we were still in St. Petersburg, Noel Reynolds, the father of one of our missionaries, sent us a thoughtful thank-you for looking out for his son. He then incidentally asked if I kept a journal and, if so, whether I would mind sharing it with him. Noel, who now serves as associate academic vice president at BYU, shared the manuscript with Dan Peterson, director of the Foundation for Ancient Research and Mormon Studies. After our return, Dan encouraged me to show it to a publisher and mentioned the work to John W. Welch, editor in chief of *BYU Studies*. John then asked me to make a presentation from my journal at the 1997 BYU Studies Academy annual meeting at the Joseph Smith Building in Salt Lake City. This presentation led to his and his editors' eventual interest in bringing it out in book form.

During the preparation of this volume, I was occasionally privileged to read a letter from a colleague or two who had meanwhile been called to preside in a Russian-speaking mission. Their vivid accounts of memorable incidents from their own experience both had a familiar ring and humbled me by the realization that probably anyone who has ever served as a mission president could have produced a book like this one.

This has led me to conjecture about the keeping of journals, so forcefully encouraged by President Spencer W. Kimball and his successors. What valuable insights have been lost to us because so relatively few of our forebears took the time to provide a record of their lives—particularly of the spiritual encounters that many so abundantly experienced. My family and I can only speculate about my great-grandfathers, all early converts and mostly émigrés. Some of their wives dictated brief memoirs toward the end of their lives, accounts that tell us at least something of their experiences, for which their vast progeny are most grateful.

Of course, some accounts of missionary activity—mostly from the early days of the Church—have been published. How impoverished we would all be without, for instance, those by Wilford Woodruff, Heber C. Kimball, Jacob Hamblin, William E. McLellin, and William Clayton. By the same token, how enriched we would be had there been even more. Although each such account is distinctive, there are also commonalities with which every returned missionary can identify. Hopefully, that will also be true of what you read in the following pages.

However, as the staff and my editor at BYU Studies have indicated, they had heretofore rarely, if at all, encountered a text like mine—subjective, anecdotal, fairly candid, yet, hopefully, inspirational as well. What may be my account's weakness as a chronology of actual events is perhaps what also sets it apart. It records not so much what occurred or *what* we did as *how it felt* to serve under the circumstances and in the capacity my wife and I and our fellow missionaries labored. I would also not be surprised if the glimpses of missionary life which follow echo the feelings and perceptions of others who have so served, or who presently do so.

The stance my journal took was not to account for my own time and effort but to record events and insights, mundane though they may seem, which struck me at the time as fairly profound. For three charmed years—summer 1993 to summer 1996—I was privileged to witness on an almost daily basis the "mighty change of heart" in missionaries and members, their heightened spiritual awareness, and the courage and heroism they mustered, even though at times they faltered, to rise above the natural man and transcend the constant adversity that accosted each of them in a variety of forms.

In particular, the journal records my personal response, my musings over those events as they occurred, mostly in others' lives, sometimes in my own. I often responded with amazement and also with a hint of my own inadequacy in comparison with those others. Those three years were truly a time of awakening and spiritual discovery. As I declare in one of the journal's segments, "Is it not an utterly inspired and ultimately win-win policy that the Lord would, by such extensive delegation, require so many of us, so ostensibly unqualified, to be trusted and, again, entrusted with the carrying forward of his sacred work—the salvation of souls?" My hope is that this and other impressions that came to me then will have some impact and significance for others also.

The selection of a title is never an easy decision. The editors and I long wrestled with an appropriate choice for this volume. I'd have given my eyeteeth for the citation from Ephesians 2:19—"No more strangers"—already used by Elder Hartmon Rector Jr. for his stirring multivolume compilation of testimonies by various converts. We also considered lines from various Church hymns. "Called to Serve" had, I was informed, already been used. Because of the journal's fairly realistic depiction of personal struggles and the desperate circumstances that prevail in today's Russia, we also thought of such otherwise obscure lines as "to a dark, benighted land" and "the dark night is o'er." Some felt the latter to be, if anything, too optimistic.

We next turned to the Book of Mormon and its stirring account of so many missionary experiences. As missionaries frequently read the Book of Mormon, they might well view it, with its panoply of role models, as primarily a manual for them. The many proselytizing moments recounted there bear an uncanny resemblance to those in our own time—which in turn witnesses to those moments' authenticity and supports Nephi's admonition that we "liken all scriptures unto us, that it might be for our profit and learning" (1 Ne. 19:23).

Alma 28:13–14—which serves as this book's epigraph—particularly reminds me of what I regard as the great equation that states the terms and conditions of this life's ultimate success or failure. It also seems to bear out my own shadowed yet light-filled depiction of the privilege that was ours and our missionaries' during the Church's first decade in Russia.

In our ongoing search for the right title, the editors and I also thought of settling for a possible phrase from the Prophet Joseph's blessing to two Apostles who, shortly before Joseph's martyrdom, were set apart to travel to Russia—which land he predicted would play a significant role in "some of the most important things concerning the advancement and building up of the kingdom of God in the last days."[1] We also thought of somehow employing a phrase culturally and historically meaningful to native Russians but less so to most of those who would tend to be our readers—"the Russian Soul." Eventually, my astute editor, Doris Dant, came up with a title that is very short and simple, hence more easily remembered. "A Call to Russia," would, we felt, best encompass all that the book might convey. Less is sometimes truly more.

In addition to the foregoing, I am especially indebted to, again, Doris Dant for the invaluable and painstaking care she has given the project since it came to her attention, as well as to her associates Karl Batdorff (a former student of mine), Heather Seferovich, and Robert Spencer. I appreciate the conscientious proofing and helpful suggestions of Marny Parkin, Christian Sorensen, Jona Tres Kap, Marilyn Olson, Alena Lauritsen, Amy Felix, and Stephanie Christensen. As with my plays and other publications, these journal entries were enthusiastically received by my colleagues in the BYU Department of Germanic and Slavic Languages and by the principal source of encouragement in all I undertake, my wife, Merriam.

Finally, my thanks to Dima Borisov, J. Preston Hughes, Mary Rogers, and the following former missionaries for so generously sharing their photos of their St. Petersburg mission: Ray Banks, Eric Blaser, John Bradshaw, Nathan Draschil, Andrew Eversole, Darin Fawcett, Gail Halvorsen, Michael Hertig, Loren Hulse, Chris James, Morgan Magleby, Marino Martin, Donald Morgan, Jon Reynolds, Chad Smith, Matt and Wendy (Bingham) Stepan, Darrel Stubbs, Brian and Jena (Hughes) Tew, and John Valentine.

The BYU Studies staff made the final selection of photographs for this volume. Their criteria included appropriate "fit" with the accompanying text, sharpness of image, good black-and-white contrast, and, wherever possible, the depiction of action rather than a static pose. Again, thanks to the many missionaries who submitted, in all, over three hundred pictures and so patiently awaited their return.

Also, special thanks to the several missionaries whose heartfelt personal accounts appear throughout this manuscript. I received many such on a weekly basis during the three years we were in Russia.

---

1. Joseph Smith Jr., *History of The Church of Jesus Christ of Latter-day Saints,* ed. B. H. Roberts (Deseret Book, 1971), 6:41.

Year One

Summer 1993
to
Spring 1994

First Impressions: Summer 1993

Rough Landing

Probably like any new mission president, I'd rehearsed in my imagination during the long flight over how I ought to feel and with what spirit I ought to embark on this weighty new assignment. I badly wanted to reflect the right mood—faith-driven self-assurance and quiet dignity—to those we would first encounter. I hoped thereafter to maintain and project that posture throughout the three years of our ministry.

Having at last landed, my wife and I headed for the baggage claim. We soon discovered that, although the other passengers had retrieved their luggage, ours was nowhere to be seen. After waiting still longer, I finally walked to an opening above the conveyer belt and peeked through the strips of rubber hanging there. On the other side—in fact outside the building—stood our suitcases with several airport workers standing by, leisurely smoking. These were clearly the same men who had just lifted the other passengers' luggage onto the conveyer. All were younger than I and, as one would expect, in better physical condition. I shouted through the opening, pointing to our luggage, "That's ours!" "It's too heavy!" came the reply.

Then something like the mood of vengeful furies took over—or was it the spirit of John Wayne in *True Grit* or *Red River?* Without further hesitation, I jumped upon the moving conveyer belt and rode it through the same opening to the loading area and the men I'd just addressed. There I leapt to the ground, lifted our admittedly quite heavy pieces onto the conveyer, and while riding with them back into the waiting room, shouted in the other direction, "Well, I suppose that shows that I'm not only older but stronger than the rest of you!"

My remark, which evoked not the slightest antagonism or shame, was met with total indifference—which infuriated me all the more. A tip was obviously all that interested those men and was what they'd been waiting for all along. Meanwhile, the new mission president's spiritual serenity, his self-assurance and quiet dignity, had dissipated with our aircraft's high-octane exhaust. An utterly ludicrous commencement, with the single and perhaps not insignificant blessing that it immediately erased any vestiges of pride or self-importance.

Two Hats

The multiple charges of this mission-related assignment will be particularly challenging—stewardship not only for the missionaries and the proselytizing program, but also for the local Church organization: the opportunity, in tandem with an impressive number of eager and experienced priesthood and auxiliary leaders, to help develop and strengthen an already-established Church entity.

Setting

As it must have been under the tsars, St. Petersburg still affords more of a contrast than probably any other Russian city. The imperial edifices—including numerous ministry buildings—are breathtakingly immense in scale, the friezes and outright sculpture of their facades opulent beyond those of such structures anywhere else. But the high-rise tenements most everyone lives in—vast tracts of them—suggest another aesthetic, which is crude if not ugly, monotonous, and barely functional.

Courtesy Andrew Eversole

View of St. Petersburg's endless high-rise apartments. During the Communist regime, St. Petersburg was renamed Leningrad. After the fall of the Soviet Union, the city's original name was restored. Residents, however, still refer to this section of the city as Leningrad.

This impression is compounded by the condition of streets and walkways everywhere, I'm told, in the later winter. I've whimsically commented that here the earth must have already received its paradisiacal glory—a sea of glass (read "treacherous ice") mined with canine excrement wherever you put down your feet. The high incidence of broken hips on the part of the many older people who fall on it and the consequent deaths from pneumonia are certainly one way to minimize the state's geriatric caseload and burden of pensioners. The health problems that plague children (due chiefly to polluted water and malnutrition) are other great population levelers. And all of this misfortune couldn't have happened to a more lovable, or in many respects a more innocent, people.

St. Petersburg's climate and its seasons are far from moderate—lately a heat wave alternating with wet, cold weather—and seem to take their toll. The summer white nights encourage people to sleep less, though we all need as much sleep as ever, and induce a kind of listlessness. With it comes an inattentiveness shown by investigators during lessons or by some members to their Church obligations. All of this coincides with the *dacha* season, when Russians traditionally spend every weekend (if not weeks on end) throughout the summer in their country gardens—not just tending their crops, but indulging in a general lethargy aided by alcohol.

When summer days are eventually displaced by the dark days of winter, an opposite but equally immoderate response takes over instead— depression in some and the urge to sleep too much. Perhaps this in turn reflects, or has to some extent shaped, those manic-depressive extremes so observable in literary characters and in the nation's history.

With essentially two additional winter months taken off to celebrate both the Orthodox and the Western Christmases and New Year's, one can surmise that many Russians spend close to half the year on vacation. How miraculous therefore that some essentially disregard such tradition, join the Church, and attend each Sunday throughout the year.

Wary

As we entered the small auditorium we'd rented for our first zone conference, all of us—missionaries we'd never seen before, Merriam, and I—were full of anxiety, our thoughts tinged with apprehension. How would we come across? How would they? Who was this new presiding couple that had so abruptly replaced the one they knew so well and felt so at home with? Would we be harsh and unreasonably demanding? Or too permissive? The introductions and personal interviews to follow would doubtless dispel any uncertainty. Then everyone would have a better sense of what to expect during the months—in some cases years—that lay before us.

And that was certainly the case—entirely dispelling any residual fear or tension and reassuring each of us that, in diligently serving the Lord, we are soon enough one, all spiritual kin, with every reason and good intention to 'be there' for one another. In fact, it was love at first sight!

Identity Crisis

Every morning Merriam still wakes up and asks, "Where am I?" while I shake off the previous night's slumber and involuntarily ask, "Who am I?"

Epiphany

To think that less than a decade ago we so feared the Russians that an American president could quip, "Let's nuke 'em!" and bumper stickers blared, "Kill a Commie for Mommy!" Of course, most of us didn't know these people, didn't recognize the preciousness of their souls, didn't perceive that they were our brothers and sisters. With relative ease we had utterly defaced them.

Great Trust

A few years back, our BYU Russian faculty got a lot of bad press from people who felt we must be communist sympathizers. Else why would we be so interested in the Russian language, culture, and people? That was one reason Gary Browning (Russian mission president, 1990–93), then I, and perhaps even our colleague Don Jarvis [who would preside over Church missions in Moscow and Ekaterinburg, 1996–99] were surprised by our calls—to realize we'd been extended that much confidence, particularly by the Brethren, if not by some others. And it's a great trust.

Echoes

Conditions here are hauntingly reminiscent of where I served my first mission—West Germany ten years after the Second World War—the same poverty and dilapidated infrastructure, the same "aping" of American culture (suddenly prestigious because we were the military-political victors), and a similar uncertainty about the nation's future. However, the Germans back then seemed more hopeful and determined to improve themselves materially by working long hours. Hence, the discouraging response most people gave us at the doorstep—*"Keine Zeit!"* ("No time!"). It isn't quite so dire here—not yet: the Russians are neither so personally driven nor so tightly organized. And they never were.

Russian Types

Our driver also serves in the office when not running errands. On our first full day, we saw a lot of him and our local district leader, who also coordinates the rental of missionary apartments. In body type and temperament, these two afford a striking contrast and resemble common stereotypes: the thin, wiry servant with quick, obsequious shuffles, who may question your judgment but never shows it, and the large-boned Misha, who, reminiscent of a Russian bear, moves toward you with a deliberately measured, more confident pace, though he is just as wily.

[Both men served the Church—and us—with unusual effectiveness and devotion. We were lucky to have our driver's services for the duration of our call. Shortly after, we learned that, true to his cautious nature, he failed one morning to show up at work without any warning. A polite note explained that by then he, his wife, and their young son would be well across the Finnish border. Still later, we learned they had immigrated to Canada.]

Family Resemblance

Yesterday was my first meeting with our assembled branch presidents, all in their best Sunday dress. Some of them, I was told, are among the charter members of the Church in Russia. But where had I seen them before—high cheek bones, mostly angular faces, distinguished beards? Yes, of course, in our literature textbooks, in a singular mid-nineteenth-century photograph of so many prominent Russian authors and critics, including both Turgenev and Tolstoy. I could even pick out my Dostoevsky, though he does not in fact appear there with the others. What a striking resemblance. But why not? Same gene pool.

A Firm Foundation

Our local leaders are so impressive. Many of them have been members for only a year or two now. Spiritually I stand in their shadow. One of the most inspiring is, appropriately, our district leader Vyacheslav Efimov. He's a dynamic, experienced leader—he supervised some five hundred transportation employees before he took his early retirement to serve the Church full time. (He must have been a trusted and able Party member earlier.) And in all he does and says, he fairly walks on spiritual clouds; he reminds me all the time that we need to pray before we transact a particular item of business. Without him the Church would be greatly diminished here unless another like him were raised up in his place.

President Efimov was well mentored, he tells me, by Gary Browning. (This is truly Gary's greatest, lasting legacy—the firm foundation he has left us here and upon which the Church can continue to build hereafter— *people,* well-trained and motivated people, fully dedicated and of the highest character, like G. B. himself. Thanks, Gary. It has made all the difference in this mission—and for us personally.)

Perhaps the ultimate requisite is a certain quality few can claim— guilelessness. And I think I see it here in a number of Russian Slavs. The eleven branch presidents are equally representative—all very humble and earnest, all very new in the Church.

Ties That Bind

Ever since we got here, Merriam's been waiting for a fax announcing the birth of our latest grandchild. Each morning, first thing, she rushes to the office machine to see what might have dropped overnight into its tray. After about two weeks, on the very first morning she forgot to inquire, the office elders delightedly announced, "It's a boy!"

Meanwhile, we've learned that when a three-year-old grandson traveled with his parents one weekend to St. George, he burst into tears after learning we wouldn't be there. His parents then explained that other cities bear the prefix "St." and the one where we are is much farther distant. Still another very young grandchild recently startled his parents with the question "When did Grandma and Grandpa die?"

Still a New Language

After many years studying and teaching Russian, I am daunted to discover a surprising number of common colloquial expressions that for some reason have until now passed me by. Not to mention a bevy of ecclesiastical

Memorable gathering. Wolfgang Paul *(center)*, LDS area representative for Russia, presents the first Russian copies of the Doctrine and Covenants to members of the St. Petersburg South District presidency. *Center:* Wolfgang Paul; *left to right:* Igor Mezentsev, Viktor Kireiko, Stas Dilevsky, Vladimir Chipkus, and Viktor Yakovlev. As a Russian army officer, Mezentsev faced Paul, then an officer in the West German army, across the Berlin Wall only a few years earlier when both were stationed in opposed sectors of that city. Dilevsky was a branch president at nineteen years of age and has since served a mission in Russia.

terms—some traditional, some borrowed from LDS tradition, for example, *Zhenskoe Obshchestvo Miloserdiya,* "female society of mercy" (Relief Society).

Uphill Battle

In all of this, I haven't mentioned the frustration involved in getting anything logistical accomplished here—like placing a simple long-distance phone call. But anyone who's ever spent time in Eastern Europe knows all about that. It's something else that never changes, really. When neophytes act surprised, I just tell them to go read anything by the author Franz Kafka—any of his depictions of confusing, self-contradictory worlds—but not to think of it as fiction. And that's all right too. It's all worth it.

Blight

Out of seventy first interviews with the missionaries, I have one grievous concern—a disastrous altercation with one extremely precocious elder. Apparently he didn't care to listen to my get-acquainted questions but wanted only my approval for his several demands, all idiosyncratic though each of them relates to the work itself. It's ironic that he's the offspring of one of my students a generation earlier, who called me just before we came here and explained about his son's innovations and the way those ideas had miffed other elders. The father hoped I would intervene, that I'd be supportive and understanding. Every day I think of this elder and shudder at how rejected I must have made him feel by failing to endorse his suggestions. I worry about our consequent poor relationship and I am at a loss to know how I can reach him. I even wonder if he wants it this way to get some kind of perverse attention or prove something to himself about himself. And then I worry that I'm further misjudging him in drawing such conclusions. With all the exhilaration and goodwill I've experienced in the presence of the other missionaries, this is a blight that utterly weighs me down, as it must him.

Versatile

Requests sneak up on us every day from every direction. Trying to be nice, you often find yourself agreeing (or almost) before you realize that what they are asking for is inappropriate. One learns, not quickly enough, how important it is to say "No" while still caring, and how often that is necessary. What, in practice, is my job description? Dispatcher, receptionist, goodwill dispenser, coordinator, mediator, crisis manager, steward to Frankfurt, autographer (every single financial transaction requires my signature), hand holder, cheerleader, friend, and occasional naysayer, if not also "caller to repentance." Not a bad job, though never ending—full of variety and plenty of personal interaction—with every transaction terribly important to whomever I'm assisting.

Who's the Servant?

Our wonderfully gregarious and utterly meticulous housekeeper, Lydia, leaves nothing out of place. The trouble is, we don't always agree with her on what the proper place may be. Therefore, on each of the mornings Lydia comes to clean, Merriam and I rise even earlier than usual and scurry about, leaving nothing that the day before was carelessly placed on a table, kitchen counter, or—perish the thought—windowsill or floor. In other words, we do much of Lydia's work in advance of her coming to be certain that later we can still find and have access to our far-too-many personal possessions.

New Digs

In two more months we'll be moving—both apartment and office—to a newly renovated building in the historical center of Old St. Petersburg—only fifteen minutes' walk from the Hermitage (former Winter Palace), where the Revolution first surfaced. In the opposite direction, it's no more than ten minutes away from the Russian Art Museum, Petersburg Philharmonic, and five-star Hotel Europe. A block farther is Nevsky Prospekt. The new site is certainly a lot more central for most of the members.

Meanwhile, in the present facility—the tunnel-like, fourth-floor wing of a hotel on the city's northern perimeter—Merriam and I each morning reexperience the almost too convenient arrangement of living quarters and office. Stepping out of our bathroom door we face, head on, any number of petitioners, waiting in the same hallway to conduct business in the adjacent office. We've learned to be properly coiffed and buttoned before emerging from our toilet. The pair of elders who were assigned to the office before our arrival and who share a bedroom farther along the same corridor are ordinarily already in place—one to handle records, the other money, both doubling as receptionists. They had all of three days' training before we arrived. We will, I suspect, be learning the ropes together.

Foot in Mouth

Shortly after our arrival, the brother that the Church engages to purchase plane fares, deliver parcels, and work with customs (I'd been told he was "in charge of transportation") reported that he'd had an accident with his personal car. He requested the use of the office van while his car got repaired. That sounded reasonable enough until, overhearing us, others drew me aside, insisting I should not have authorized the personal use of Church property. The Russian proverb "Everyone carries his own suitcase" was also duly invoked. It only then became clear that, in this case, "transportation" meant something other than having access to the van. Recognizing the correctness of this insistent counsel, I thereupon approached the first party, still in the office, and rescinded permission.

Feeling somehow used, inept, and lectured to, I vented my frustration, asking in an unnaturally shrill tone, "Who's in charge here anyway?" I could immediately see the shock, if not horror, in all their faces. "What sort of choleric weirdo have we got to put up with for the next three years?" was clearly what I read there. I then and there vowed to myself to have a longer fuse in the future, whatever the circumstances.

President Thomas Rogers and District President Vyacheslav Efimov at a social for mission leaders. Efimov served as a friend and confidant, helping Rogers understand the Russian people and culture.

President Efimov has rescued me more than once since then as various petitioners have come by with desperate and, as it turns out, deceptive ploys to wrest from the Church charitable funds I do not have and am not authorized to spend. One was a woman who had merely spoken once with the missionaries on a street corner, obtaining through them the office address and phone number. She was after money to make the apartment she rented "just plain livable." President Efimov and his wife had even visited her, determining in the process that she was illegally residing in the city, hence technically ineligible to be a renter.

Fortunately, the last (but not only) time she thereafter telephoned to harangue us for pretending to be Christians, President Efimov was on hand. It took me a minute or so after laying down the receiver to find and then persuade him to listen to the woman's vindictive diatribe. She was meanwhile still going strong, clearly unaware that no one had been listening during the interval. Gently lifting the receiver, President Efimov verified who it was and how intense her unabating monologue was; then, after a few seconds, he chimed in with a soft "Uh-huh" and hung up, as I should have much earlier.

On another occasion a young inactive member I'd never met before insisted his wife would shortly die without our advancing a certain high sum for an operation. Again, President Efimov was on hand. He calmly asked for further details, indicating we would need to verify the wife's condition with the doctors and that, if indeed we were in a position to assist, payment would be made directly to the hospital. The man immediately backed off and, I learned some time later, confessed that the whole thing had been a hoax—an attempt to get money for some heavy drinking.

Bottom Line

We've been especially touched by the wholeheartedness of the Saints here and of so many missionaries—which is ultimately a reflection of their profound faith. That primary condition and first principle becomes, after all, a fundamental gauge of everything else.

True Grit

Merriam has quickly come to know and draw close to a number of sisters and female investigators. Last Saturday she felt the need to attend one such investigator's baptism. I had to be elsewhere with the mission van and driver. The difficulty is we've been here only a few weeks—not even months yet—and Merriam's language skills are sparse, her acquaintance with the city's topography still more limited. But armed with only her passport, subway fare, and as clear a map as the elders could draw her, Merriam nevertheless headed alone into Petersburg's busy traffic. If she became lost, she'd be virtually unable to make out directional signs or understand what well-intended passersby might try to explain. She got to the baptism though and returned intact.

This particular baptism, held in a public park on the shores of a large lake, attracted a number of curious swimmers, who momentarily interrupted their crawl or sidestroke to float and stare. No doubt the service provided one of their more fascinating ventures into the water. Merriam's solitary journey to the lake and back was itself an exciting and memorable plunge into her own deep water.

Heavy Duty

The St. Petersburg airport has begun to feel like our second home. It is located at the exact opposite end of the city from the *Chaika* Hotel. We visit the airport every second week or so. That often we either meet a new group of elders and sisters or bring several to their plane as they complete their missions. We do the same for visiting General Authorities and Church personnel from either our area headquarters in Frankfurt or from Salt Lake City.

St. Petersburg has no beltway, so each time we must travel through the city's congested center and contend with heavy traffic all the way. By Western standards the airport is extremely austere: few chairs, no indoor heat in cold weather (which is all but three months out of the year), long delays retrieving baggage and passing through customs, and no view of landings or of arriving guests until they spill into the airport building's amazingly small, lone outer lobby (which services all flights and all airlines).

The inconvenience entailed by our frequent travel and long waiting is just symptomatic of the many hardships most Russians have had to put up with throughout their lives. People in the West have little if any comprehension of these adversities.

Time Warp

The lawlessness here increasingly reminds us of what we read about Chicago gangsterism in the thirties (if not also the gangsterism now current in Los Angeles, the Bronx, and Washington, D.C.), while we are further reminded that the Church here has the same youth and innocence and potential for growth that it did in New York and Kirtland in the early thirties a century earlier.

Settling In: Autumn 1993

Fun House

It's a wonder that anyone without a liahona can find the mission office or our apartment in the Chaika (Seagull) Hotel. Not only is the Chaika located on a remote side street at the far northwest end of town, but its own circuitous corridors also encompass a labyrinth of twists and turns through a succession of annexes, wings, and tacked-on additions. En route one encounters a welter of lobbies with gift shops, a hairdresser's, and more.

Cultural and Affective Deficits

As I'm beginning to suspect, many of St. Petersburg's adult population—highly qualified pedagogues, former rocket engineers, and computer technicians—were for seventy-four years and four successive generations deprived not only of any viable religious or philosophical indoctrination but also of any serious or sophisticated acquaintance with even their own great literature and the humanities, which still seem to some of them superfluous and decadent, if not diabolic. (So all that wonderful Russian literature, so accessible and affordably priced through Soviet bookstore outlets in the U.S. throughout the Cold War, was, one assumes, mostly for export and external, propagandistic consumption.) This was surely as oppressive and tyrannical a policy as what was done to undermine the people's material well-being and in some cases their very physical existence. At any rate, among those I've encountered thus far, there is seemingly little tolerance for various opinions or interpretations of the same text. People discount the possibility that differing viewpoints are not necessarily in opposition but can together enrich one's total perspective.

Nor did Marxist indoctrination noticeably develop parental accountability in many contemporary Russians. From the November 1 *Moscow Times:*

> Child Abuse Takes Up to 200,000 Lives: Up to 200,000 Russian children die every year from injuries received at home, many caused by violence or neglect by their parents, a member of parliament said Tuesday. Painting a grim picture of violence, poverty and social disintegration in post-communist Russia, Maria Gaidash told the newspaper *Nezavisimaia Gazeta* that about 2 million children under 14 suffered physical or mental damage at home every year. "Up to 10 percent of them die," she said. Gaidash, a member of the Women of Russia party in the State Duma,

15

said about 50,000 children fled their homes each year and at least 2,000 killed themselves rather than face domestic misery.

Bipolar

The manic-depressive extremes in the Russian national character, which the philosopher Nikolay Berdyaev spoke of, are clearly manifest here, though it is hard to know if they are innate or just a symptom of continuing hard times. Already I have personally encountered emotional responses that knew no bounds in the depth of their gloom or in their unabated hysteria. Such encounters lead me to wonder if I have not reentered one of Dostoevsky's novels. He really didn't make it up, and what we sometimes think was his peculiar temperament is more widespread than one might imagine.

Alternatives

In their outlook, many here—deprived until three years ago of the opportunity to consider and choose what to believe and how to behave—are still like pre-Fall Edenites, innocent and fragile. Those who deal with them, tread lightly! In contrast to prevailing religious traditions (whatever their aesthetic and emotional appeal), the restored Church and its teachings embrace vivid light rather than darkness, sociability instead of introversion, life rather than death, happiness instead of sorrow. Although these boons come to us through God's grace, they must of course also be worked for.

Universal

It is a tremendous witness that, in the lives of their Russian adherents, the restored gospel and the Church are so viable. That there are any adherents whatsoever in this otherwise historically alien setting—with its longstanding state religions, first Orthodoxy, then atheistic Communism—is indeed a great witness to the restored gospel's universal significance and appeal.

Angels

There are beacons here—"temples" in their own right—that with their very presence sufficiently signal and draw others to the light that undeniably radiate from them. These include most missionaries, as well as those extraordinary converts who come from who knows where and so overwhelm us. Even if in each branch they are relatively few, taken together they're an impressive host. I have no better term for them than *angel*, which in Greek simply means "messenger." And—with their total, unwavering trust and commitment; their earnestness; their warm, sunny, caring disposition; their confident joy—what a message they deliver!

Gospel Dynamics

As early as the first week or so—as jet lag slowly began to recede—it seemed we had been into this assignment forever. I think every missionary feels this way. A mission takes hold and immediately defines him or her. The missionary instinctively avoids thinking too wistfully or nostalgically about other times and places—daydreaming, that is—whereas back home, while still in school, he or she did so all the time: "Who shall I date?" "What courses should I take next semester?" "What career should I pursue?"

Like few other life events, there is something all-consumingly present about the mission experience. It is that intense and, I'm persuaded, is meant to be so. A wonderful training or practicum—a laboratory, apprenticeship, testing. One can hardly remain the same in the face of such involvement and exposure.

Most new members are required to change at least as radically. But what a miraculous phenomenon—what a lift to otherwise complacent, plateaued adult lives—to have two dark-suited messengers appear at your door and through their instrumentality be challenged to become something you had heretofore never consciously imagined but whose benefit becomes immediately apparent.

The long-held opinion of many philosophers and social critics that God is dead and religion no longer relevant totally ignores both our investigators' deeply felt yearning for a more purposeful life and the way the restored gospel in so many instances addresses that desire. The extremes of human suffering and the lack of personal fulfillment, however unwished for, dictate that one humbly holds onto ancient verities.

By Study As Well As by Faith

Merriam says she's become a "street junky." The expression would be hard to explain and impossible to translate. By it, she means that since reading a useful guidebook she can readily identify the name of whichever canal we happen to pass in any part of the city. That's because the ornate grillwork that adorns every canal has, in each case, its own special design. Our otherwise astute driver and other native Petersburgers, who've passed these canals for a lifetime, are astounded when, as we drive about the city, Merriam calls out the names of canals they can't identify.

By Chance?

Last night, a dynamic branch president, Vyacheslav Kondratev, asked me if I believed that anything at all is really governed by chance. I hesitated to answer. President Kondratev, who is reinforced by what I've already witnessed here, has managed to persuade me that all obstacles and rebuffs serve a spiritual purpose. They are tailored to our need for further growth. We should therefore accept them, whatever form they take, and allow others all the time and space they may need to do the same. Kondratev is quite a philosopher, while Efimov is more a pragmatist with loads of common sense and wisdom concerning the ways of the world. Both have as much faith and devotion as I have ever seen—a wonderful team. [Vyacheslav Kondratev later became a district president.]

True Fellowship

Another reason Russians may "take" to our message more than many other nationalities do—they've been so polarized by adverse social forces that, having only the smallest circle of close family and friends, they are that much hungrier for the social involvement the Church has to offer, including the fellowship of God himself.

Touch-Up

We've decided to recommend changing the names of several branches that, reflecting the major thoroughfares in their area, unwittingly honor various revolutionary heroes—"murderers," as one of our leaders put it.

James Bond

Two emergency trips to Frankfurt for payroll. The local Russian bank appears unable to accept money transfers anymore. Perhaps they can't get

Courtesy Gail Halvorsen

Vyacheslav Kondratev and Elder Steven Scrogham. Kondratev served as a branch president and, more than any other member, is remembered by missionaries for his enthusiasm for the gospel and his total dedication to Church service.

hold of the Western currency to disburse to us. Or perhaps they're a Mafia operation and have simply pocketed the approximately thirty thousand dollars that we know has been forwarded to our account by now. The amount I brought back both times on my person, had it been known, would for some have been sore temptation to commit murder.

Others' Burdens

It helps to remember the many good people who put up with and made the best of the Soviet regime when they had no choice in the matter. They persisted in serving one another then as best they could (some as Party members) rather than murmuring too much. I think of them with admiration; a number of them are now some of our finest, most committed members.

Skin Deep

A choice example of St. Petersburg's opulence is Oranienbaum (renamed Lomonosov in the Soviet era), another tsarist estate to the south of and on the same train line as the town of Pushkin and of the Romanovs' most grandiose summer palace. Oranienbaum's exquisite Chinese Palace (*Kitaisky Dvorets*), just one of several such buildings in its complex, is also one of the few royal residences that was not severely damaged in World War II. Many of its rooms display original eighteenth-century parquet floors and embroidered wall coverings in astoundingly fine condition.

We had gone there on a preparation day with our office staff. On the grounds of the *Kitaisky Dvorets*, we had admired a large cast-iron replica of the famous ancient Greek *Laocoon*, which poignantly depicts the destruction of a father and his sons in the coils of a divinely vengeful python. We had praised the work's dramatic composition and its evocation of powerful emotions.

A few days later on the way from the airport, my assistants and I encountered something similar. We had met six new missionaries and, loaded with their luggage, were on our way with them to the mission home. On this occasion, we had already encountered at least one drunk lying on a curb and another about to collapse. We then saw what we were truly not prepared for. As the mission van slowed, then halted during a bottleneck in the traffic, we noticed yet another man kneeling opposite us on the sidewalk. He cradled in his arms the head of an older man, gray and balding, who lay prone before him. The latter, whatever his condition, had clearly sustained enough physical shock that he was no longer in control of his bladder. What we at first thought was blood had noticeably issued from his body and streamed across the dry cement into the nearby gutter.

Standing next to them was a woman his approximate age, doubtless the victim's wife. She stood mute, looking desperately, if not hopelessly, about her. A second younger man, less passive and clearly part of the same tableau, agitatedly waved his arms and called out to the cars ahead of us, including an ambulance with closed curtains. Still a third, even younger man—another of this Laocoon's sons—had darted into the street and with his fists beat upon the windows of several cars to get their drivers' attention. All to no avail.

With our keen but arrested aesthetic detachment, not unlike what had been aroused in us at Oranienbaum, we sensed the scene's strong pathos as we and the cars ahead of us eventually drove on. As we did so, the analogy of the parable of the Good Samaritan was surely not lost on any of us—nor the dawning realization that, like each of the other drivers, we had played the pharisaical role.

What had prevented my asking at least a row of our new elders and one of my assistants to leave the van and proceed to the mission home by subway? Their seats could have easily accommodated the old man and woman. Or did he already seem too hopeless, too far gone? And were we just too unsure where to take him? Or whether the nearest hospital or clinic would even admit him without the right credentials? Or was it simply that he was too old and no longer counted for much? Or that his bodily fluids would mess our van? Or that our driver, with his own strong fatalistic views, might object? Or that the man, being a nondescript Russian and doubtless a nonmember, was one of "them" and really not one of "us"—he was supposed to endure whatever fate held in store for him because he was less "special" where we were concerned, less "deserving?"

Our motives in passing the man by—particularly mine, as I more than anyone was in a position to call the shots—haunt me still and raise larger questions: Just how qualified are we to represent the Savior here? And of what value is his "salt" when it loses its "savor?"

Communist agitation. Russian men and women gather outside Gostiny Dvor, St. Petersburg's largest department store, advocating the old order.

Just a day or so later, during my stroll to a nearby park, I encountered yet another man lying completely inert next to a curb, but the man was still breathing and presumably drunk. You see such every day. This time I took the trouble to alert others, who assured me they would call for help—probably the police. It was getting cold, and should the man lie there all night he might easily die of exposure.

We battle to get out of our own skin. With our move of both office and residence at the time of the bloody political crisis in Moscow (Yeltsin's firing on his opponents in the Russian White House) and our subsequent inability to watch TV or listen to the radio, we were fairly impervious to what was happening there, to the now over two hundred deaths.

Out of Touch

To transfer to new quarters, we had to use professional movers. We were warned to have elders stationed at every portal to and from the vans to discourage pilfering. Meanwhile, our phones and fax were disconnected for a number of days so that we had an almost total news blackout. Intently listening to their shortwave radios, several Church members tried to update us, but we were really too busy to pay much notice. Had there been a serious emergency—a call to evacuate the country—we'd have been hard to reach. However, as on so many previous occasions, the dust has finally settled, and the nation's life proceeds in its usual placid, though still chaotic, fashion.

Well Appointed

At the time of our move to the new mission apartment—in a completely restored edifice dating from the time of Pushkin and just a block down fashionable Moika Street from the great author's final residence (now the Pushkin House Museum)—I was tempted to protest, "No, at our own additional expense, we'll find quarters more like what most Russians have to settle for—a shabby, cramped set of rooms in one of the typically dingy high rises that are everywhere around us. We'll come to the missionary apartment for special occasions and to receive guests but otherwise try to 'fit in' better with the prevailing living standard and lifestyle." But the flesh is weak, and perhaps, we rationalized, our presence in such a prestigious neighborhood would, in the eyes of both the public and the members, lend the Church a certain desirable respectability.

Courtesy Andrew Eversole

New mission home *(second building from the right)* beside the Moika River Canal. The name *Moika* is derived from the Russian verb meaning to wash. Tsarist cavalry, whose former barracks faced the mission home, bathed their horses at this point in the river. The mission home and office share a restored edifice with the South African and French consulates as well as Rothman's Tobacco—strange bedfellows indeed.

Deceived

On many mornings since the move and the onset of cold weather, we'd marveled at the wispy white clouds that rushed past our fifth-story apartment window. The prevailing Baltic winds must, we assumed, be particularly swift and constant. That was until, more recently, we figured it out: the clouds are just white steam from the chimney of an adjacent building.

Avant Garde

The elders in charge of baptisms come to our apartment each week for a fresh supply of baptismal clothes. These Merriam launders after their return. Each week's new order is packed in a large duffel bag that the elders carry while traveling to the baptism on the metro (subway). This week there was no laundry. En route to their apartment after the latest baptism, an elder momentarily set down the duffel bag. When he stooped to pick it up before entering the metro, it had disappeared. If next summer we spot someone dressed all in white, we'll at least know who just couldn't resist absconding with the latest high fashion in summer apparel.

One True Christian

As we visited the missionaries in Vyborg a week or so ago, we encountered one of the very first missionaries to serve in Russia. He was back on a visit. He's been credited with having brought in fifty or more of the first members there. At the time of our visit, he was being feted by some of the sisters in one of their apartments, and I have never witnessed such closeness and camaraderie among a gathering of Church members.

The former missionary, whose name is John Webster, had a presence about him that helped us understand why he'd so endeared himself to the Vyborg members. He was utterly self-effacing and calmly focused on others. As he accompanied us back to our hotel, we suddenly noticed he'd lagged behind to allow a particularly repulsive old beggar woman to wheedle money from him. The rest of us had instinctively evaded her. I thought she might even be a man (mustache and all) and was sure she was a "professional," stationing herself just then outside the city's only Western tourist hotel. But Webster didn't seem to notice as we watched and wondered why by now he wasn't more worldly wise. It was, however, *he* who gave *us* pause as we watched him, still oblivious to his audience, hand her 200 rubles and then kiss her hairy cheek. The members call him John the Baptist, but at that moment I thought I had seen the Savior or one of his truest disciples.

Palpable

There is a difference in how the Russian members testify—they assert Christ's divinity less (I suspect they take it for granted) and witness more what they have deeply felt of the Holy Spirit. Less reasoning, more feeling.

Metamorphosis

Our common acceptance of the restored gospel and our mutual involvement in the Church enable us to know and love one another on a fundamental level of respect and goodwill we could never otherwise approach.

Witness the tender, caring response of nineteen-year-old missionaries toward others, including the elderly, so untypical of the otherwise macho, self-absorbed young adult years.

A Hard Life

The present generation of Russian children are largely unhealthy, and when you know something about their drinking water alone, there's little wonder. Perhaps socialism's most damning legacy is the genocide of future generations, the offspring of the very people who were supposed to bring the system forward.

The belated reportage on Chernobyl's victims: 18 percent, a Russian newspaper now says, took their own lives after falling ill to radiation. Inadequate nutrition and carcinogenic water practically everywhere. Deficiently heated, ever-deteriorating buildings and living quarters, decaying infrastructure. It spills over as injustice and rank deception at all social levels, to which in their resigned way the Russians apply the term *ispytanie* (trial) and which may in turn account for their remarkable spirituality in the Dostoevskian sense ("salvation through suffering"). Every day one encounters here further instances of mid-nineteenth-century social evils, of Dostoevsky's spiritual milieu, of his characters' hysteria and depression.

Catalyst

I have the sense that, wherever you may find them in this world, "islands" of extraordinary caring on the part of one person (or group) for another are valid conduits of the Spirit. The Church enables people to extend themselves in this way far more broadly and less arbitrarily in both time (ancestors and progeny) and space (all presently living). Brought to that process are those who at first are not necessarily inclined or who otherwise lack the opportunity to practice such caring.

Become the Message

An elder shared with me a letter from his elders quorum president, who wrote:

> The challenging task is for you as a missionary to become the message. People who are seeking truth should be able to look into your eyes and see it. People who are seeking Christ's love should be able to sit with

you in a room and feel it. Get close enough to the Lord until people as well as Satan are forced to say, "The force is strong in this one."

Jockeying

In the company of Dmitry Silchenkov, the Church's Russian attorney, and Elder Robert K. Dellenbach of our Area Presidency, I've just returned from another goodwill visit with Mr. K., the city's official director of religious affairs. Mr. K. earlier served the Soviet government in a similar capacity, which strongly suggests that he was a Party member and is a nonbeliever. That may be a good thing, however. When periodically invited to Mr. K.'s offices together with the representatives of various other minority faiths—each eyeing the others warily—I know we are all on equal ground.

It's not very high ground, though. Mr. K. hears our concerns and receives petitions, promising to pass them forward to the mayor's council. He then assures us that we are known and our congregations still tolerated. We always leave such sessions more anxious than before to remain in the good graces of Mr. K. and the city fathers. Which, I suspect, is exactly what they have in mind.

Courtesy Donald Morgan

Role Models

Tuesday night is, for me, perhaps the single most inspiring moment in the week. As I wait to meet with our district leaders after their long workday and cross-town trek to the office, I begin to worry and ask myself, "Will they come this time? And why should they? What's in it for them?" No one

Role models: Andrey Semyonov (*left*) and Donald Morgan, the mission's first seminary and institute supervisor. Semyonov is an unassuming physician who faithfully served for seven years as the principal priesthood leader in Vyborg. The Semyonovs were the first Russian family to be sealed in the temple, and he is the first Russian this century to receive the Melchizedek Priesthood.

in their society—neighbors, co-workers, and often not even the members of their family—expects it of them or much understands. But they come, and I must pinch myself before again recognizing why: because they believe in the work. Because they have testimonies as firm and motivating as any that you will encounter anywhere.

Great Trust

The trust mission presidents are extended is an amazing thing. (Doubtless the Brethren feel the same way about their callings, but more profoundly, I imagine.) It motivates us like nothing else to want to be accountable and to do well. Should we not take a cue from this by trusting one another more—as the Lord manifestly trusts (at least entrusts) all his children to be, say, parents, however unfit many are? (And could there be any greater trust than that?) Is it not an utterly inspired and ultimately win-win policy that the Lord would, by such extensive delegation, require so many of us, who are so ostensibly unqualified, to be trusted and, again, entrusted with the carrying forward of his sacred work—the salvation of souls?

Secular Temples

Clearly, the mission has done nothing to dampen my aesthetic enthusiasms—and prejudices. (Can I help it if we were assigned to this cultural Mecca?) Happily, the simple goodness of so many—like our missionaries, who tend to enjoy superficial spectacle (i.e., action films and musicals), and a number of the members who are quite indifferent to the high art that emerged in the very city of their birth—is equally overwhelming.

Few of them take the muses as seriously as I, so they are less distracted by those secular temples of concert hall, museum, and theatre. Or is the department store sometimes a crude equivalent for us all? Is what comes out of it what matters most? *Tovary* (goods) are increasingly abundant here, if you can afford them, and their acquisition is as strong a deterrent to sacrifice and service to the Lord as any opposing ideology.

Standing Amazed: Winter 1994

Challenge

Slick ice now coats the sidewalks beneath a deceptive inch or two of fresh snow. You can't go far these days without seeing someone suddenly lose balance and take a hard fall. Conditions are especially serious for the elderly, though many a little old lady still goes out each day to purchase her daily fare. Like so many young people, one such lady, an acquaintance, even delights in taking a few small running steps, then bracing herself for a long, precarious glide. This, of course, leaves an exposed and treacherous path for those who come after.

Despite our caution and our strained effort to remain upright, Merriam and I have both had a bad fall or two already. In defense, Merriam has developed what she calls her "E.T. waddle." It adds twenty minutes more to any errand, but she at least returns without any broken bones. So far.

Winter Idyll

Plant life adorns itself with vivid blooms in spring and summer, then with equally vibrant multicolored leaves in autumn. But it takes the eight-month-long winter to bring out, through their garb, the individuality and style consciousness of Russians. The women are absolutely svelte in their generally well-tailored, warm overcoats. And both they and most men, young and old, begin to reveal their true alter egos when they don their unrestrained fur headgear (*shapki*). Our missionaries follow suit. Now all are birds on display, many a peacock among them. Fair compensation for the otherwise dark, dull winter. Animal rights activists, please look the other way. The fur hats here aren't just a superfluity. Without them few Russians could survive these northern winters.

The snows that attend winter manage, incidentally, to conceal a multitude of eyesores—muddy ruts and potholes, clutter and debris, scarred and defaced surfaces. They truly transform St. Petersburg into the ethereal, frosted dreamland it must have been in Pushkin's day. The kingdom of winter snow is like the setting of some initiatory ceremony to which all—Brueghel-like—slowly, cautiously plodding through it, are now subject. In their heavy, body-heat-preserving garb, all are suppliants—all one. In this season, Russia truly comes into her own. Winter seems her proper element, and, surprisingly, I would rather spend it here, like a Russian, than anywhere else I can imagine.

The Neva River across from the Hermitage. The Neva River freezes over in midwinter, when it can be traversed by foot. However, numerous drownings occur in early spring when the reckless or unwary continue to cross the thawing river.

Give Us This Day

For decades now, in this still essentially peasant society, the art of bread making has been relegated to the State. Bread prices were kept artificially low throughout the Soviet period, and the staff of life is still highly subsidized by the Russian government. People are less inclined to riot if they can at least fill their stomachs.

When we went today to the local bread store, as usual, a long, serpentine line had formed both inside and outside the shop. Snow and mud were tracked everywhere on its old dirty floorboards. Then I saw something I'd not witnessed before—a dispute between two men about who was first in line. A small thing, but something that quickly escalated into raised fists and loud curses. Most everyone else just looked the other way, which said to me that for all of them the incident had recurred many times in the past and that the best way was not to get involved. The Soviet Russian version of road rage?

Against All Odds

From Elder Paul Anderson:

Last August, Elder Richard Turpin and I went contacting on Grazhdansky Prospect. As it was Monday, however, there were not many people on the street, and our success was minimal. So when a young family of three came into sight, Elder Turpin and I jumped on them. Of course, as the father told me later, they had seen us from a mile or more away. Our white shirts and ties gave us away instantly as foreigners, and they thought we were lost and simply wanted help. How mistaken they were.

However, our broken Russian did not help. I had been in the country for eight months, and Elder Turpin for less than three. In fact, only Tanya, the mother, understood anything we tried to say. I would say something, and she would transcribe it from missionary Russian into real Russian.

Of course, Tanya was probably more ready for our message. A few days earlier, she had mentioned to her husband, Igor, that in spite of their having all they needed, something was still missing in their lives. She thought it was religion.

We showed them the Book of Mormon, gave them the address to the Ploshchad Muzhestva Branch, and invited them to attend. For the Tarasovs, 11:00 A.M. was much too early to get up on a Sunday. Yet for some reason, both Tanya and Igor woke up on time and came to church.

After sacrament meeting, they found us and invited us to their home. Then they waited. . . and waited. . . and waited, but we never showed. So a week passed, and they came to church again. We set up a time to meet, and then again they waited. . . and waited, and again we didn't come. Another week passed, and they came to church again. This time we set up a visit for directly after church so there could be no forgetting and no delay. With my new companion, Elder Seth Campbell, I taught them the first discussion. As Igor explains it, there was a feeling there that allowed them to trust us. It was this feeling that had brought them to church that first Sunday and prompted them to invite us to their home.

Sadly, after three discussions, we were transferred to the Petro-gradsky Branch. I called and explained to the Tarasovs that we wouldn't be there for the next discussion. That was difficult for us all. To make matters worse, when Elder Campbell and I moved out of the apart-ment, I accidentally left the keys inside. Elders Roderic Buttimore and Grant Beckwith were locked out on the very day for which I had scheduled a discussion with the Tarasovs in the missionary apartment.

What might have been a tragedy actually turned out to be a blessing, though. Elder Buttimore called and explained the situation, and Igor offered to help. A few minutes later, both he and Tanya arrived on the scene, and Igor, a professional carpenter, proceeded to take the entire door apart. Eventually, they all got in, but when Elder Buttimore offered to conduct the promised discussion, the Tarasovs declined. They thought Elder Buttimore, who is a very proper Englishman, was just too serious. Yet, as the Tarasovs soon discovered, Elder Buttimore was just as thoughtful and kind as all the rest—if not more so.

At their next appointment, Elder Buttimore asked them to be baptized. We had already scheduled them for September 20; however, the Tarasovs failed to mention this to Elder Buttimore—probably because they had never known about it. How could I have set a baptismal date without letting the Tarasovs know about it? Of course, their forgiving and staying with us after we had failed to show up for two appointments is also rather unbelievable. And everyone knows I have never been *prak-tichny* [practical]; in fact I am very often *rasseyany* [distracted].

The Tarasovs eventually agreed to a date in October. The Sunday before, Igor received a real answer to his prayers. After several nights of asking for a surer testimony of the truthfulness of our message, he sat with Tanya and Alyosha, his son, in sacrament meeting. Igor saw a distinct glow above President Kondratev, the district president, who was sitting on the stand. The glow lasted for several seconds, and even Tanya noticed it. Igor felt it was the Lord saying that baptism was the right thing for them.

On October 3, all three Tarasovs were baptized. Elder Beckwith baptized Igor, Elder Campbell baptized Alyosha, and I, Tanya. Elder Buttimore conferred the gift of the Holy Ghost upon each of them. A month and a half later, Igor was called as a counselor in the district presidency.

The Tarasovs' conversion story is quite amazing, if only because of all the silly things I did that might have kept them from being converted. Maybe the delays were a test to prove whether they really wanted to receive this blessing. Maybe not. All the same, the Lord is in charge, and if he wants the truth to reach his children who are seeking it, they will receive it.

Great Backup

The mission has two nonmember employees—and that's probably as it should be. I'm thinking of our local lawyer, Dmitry, and our maid, Lidiya. Both serve us well, and neither has much occasion to gossip with the members about the sums the Church must pay for this or that item or about our personal effects or what we eat or how well we keep our private quarters. We also have a team of security guards who control the traffic to and from our compound. One of them, Valentin, is fairly old, but he greets us with a radiant face. I can visualize him only as a high priest, perhaps officiating in the temple. That's where he belongs.

The Real Thing

From Elder Loren Hulse:

> This week I was afforded an insight into the Russian soul. Those of us in the office were still hard at work when your meeting with the district presidents let out. President Efimov cornered me by the copy machine and began to talk. He told me about the miracle of his conversion through the love and patience of his wife. He told me what communism had done to Russian fathers—how fathers now "presided" in the home by drinking and watching soccer on TV. He mourned over these counterfeit "heads of the household" and about the counterfeit priesthood leadership to which the people are accustomed. In doing so, he taught me about the power and significance of true principles. "Those who have the truth are at peace," he added. "They do not argue."

Musings

A heady whirlwind of stimulus and challenge—with no day very predictable or similar to the next. And with so many missionaries and members and investigators who are truly the *elect* of God, weak and imperfect as each of us at times is. The mutual caring, the willingness to sacrifice and be less self-referential—that is all so good and needful and inspiring. And it happens in his Church as, it seems to me, nowhere else.

Another thought: I've several times likened religion versus aesthetics and philosophical contemplation versus physical pleasure, or other seeming contraries, to the individual chips in a mosaic. Without losing their identity, they complement each other and contribute to an overall pleasing and properly balanced picture. Or, as Joseph Smith put it, "by proving contraries, truth is made manifest" (*History of the Church*, 6:428). Such a picture is what we must in many instances settle for—at least until all things shall be reconciled into one great whole.

Brave New World

Some poignant quotations from several local tenth-grade students, asked to prognosticate their future ten years hence:

- 15-year-old girl: "In a family the husband should be the most important, but the opinions of even the youngest will be heard."
- 16-year-old girl: "I should write that the stores have everything and there aren't any lines, but in my eyes that's not the most important thing. It seems to me that in the future there will be a greater appreciation for spiritual values."
- 16-year-old boy: "My work is of such a high standard that I am unrivaled. I strive to organize my business. Five years of working experience allows me to accomplish a lot. In general, life is difficult. And our wishes don't always come true. Because of this, one must above all remain sane and not show anger."
- 15-year-old boy: "The economic situation in the country is not much better than the ecological situation. The stores are completely empty. Almost all the State businesses have been destroyed or closed, and private ones are struggling to exist, so the country has not entirely collapsed. Naturally there was a sharp rise in crime. It is impossible to breathe in the city, and the water in the Neva and Lake Ladoga is heavily polluted. One can buy clean water only for huge amounts of money. The majority of the intelligent and talented people left the country. We probably will also leave soon. Our son's health is worsening, but he must continue his studies, and our country doesn't have any good schools."
- 15-year-old girl: "Life keeps getting more costly. My husband has begun to work two shifts. Each year the city becomes a little dirtier. Transportation is bad and scarce because there isn't enough gas. Broken trams and buses lie abandoned on the roads. In the city, a lot of businesses are closing because their old machinery has broken down, and there isn't the hard currency to buy new equipment. The hospital where I work together with my husband is considered one of the best in the city. One of the senior doctors has contacts in Japan, and they supply us with medicine. We do everything possible in the hospital to help people." (*Neva News*, September 15–30, 1993)

All the Difference

Christmas is for most everyone a season of nostalgic reunion with family and friends and special excitement for the very young. It is also a time when those with less firm ties are, by contrast, particularly lonely.

This is no less so in Russia, where the almost perpetual darkness is compensated for by increased attendance at concerts, the theater, and ballet as well as extended festivity. Unfortunately, in a country whose consumption of alcohol is already one of the very highest, heavy drinking also invariably attends such dark winter distractions. With fellow workers and old friends constantly toasting converts who have only recently overcome their drinking, it stands to reason that some would lapse.

One such, a relatively young man, has reverted to his former alcoholic ways. His condition, which involves self-destructive impulses, is particularly serious. Knowing this, his priesthood leaders—also relatively new to the Church—have nevertheless instinctively agreed that the young man requires special tending. So, until he has once more managed to overcome his addiction, they've decided to take turns sitting with him in his impoverished apartment and constraining his frequent attempts to resort to the bottle and to then throw himself in despair from the balcony outside his window.

This man's home teachers and the brethren in both his district and branch presidencies are as busy as we are back home at this time of year. But for a week already, on a rotating basis, each of them has found the time to be with their unfortunate brother. And that has thus far made all the difference.

Hot and Cold

Our first missionwide youth conference was held in the chilling midwinter at an outlying sports complex, formerly an off-limits military facility. We came there on a Sunday for the testimony meeting; we did not have to stay overnight in the cold barracks like the youth and their leaders. But as the one presiding, I was asked to sit for those two hours facing the others. Directly behind me was an immense single-pane window. I should have put my coat on at that point. The testimonies, so warm and vibrant, still could not moderate the steady subzero draft that penetrated my back. I left that event afflicted with what proved to be the flu and a severe bronchial infection. In the future on such occasions, I'll keep my coat on and not stand on ceremony. For all that, the exposure to our impressive young people—ninety in all—was worth it.

Fullness

I have the uncanny sense that it is not we nor our words nor even our spirit that so persuades others but the message itself, a message which is so appropriate to their feelings of personal inadequacy and need. Something else also witnesses to them, through us, even when we ourselves do not so fully feel it. It's everything that, though invisible, is nevertheless so palpable and, when deeply felt, so edifying: the Spirit, an understanding of who one really is, an eternal perspective on life's ultimate potential, an appreciation for the reality and efficacy of Christ's Atonement. Their grateful, reverent response, their eagerness to commit themselves, when commitment does occur, makes us particularly aware of what it is we are representing to them.

Courtesy Wendy Bingham Stepan

Witnessing with the Spirit. Sister Wendy Bingham (Stepan) introduces the Book of Mormon to a Russian man she has stopped on a busy street.

What's Right

From Elder Christopher Eastland:

When it's cold on the street and no one seems to want to hear your message, there's a natural tendency to be weighed down in sorrow for the people. These are some of the most trying times, when it is most difficult to be excited about the work. There is only one thing that keeps me going during those tough times—my deep conviction of the truthfulness of the work. I never tire of repeating to myself one simple phrase: "No matter what, *you* know that you're doing what's right."

Undeniable Joy

Testimony from a missionary who didn't think he had one:

> What in this world do I really know? I know feelings. They're actually more tangible and real than anything else. I especially know joy and happiness and even the hope for such in eternity. I haven't seen the gospel make immense changes in people's lives since I've been here. But when I imagine nonmember friends of mine joining the Church and picture their faces full of joy, that's when I have a knowledge of the truthfulness of the gospel and of the Church. I know they would be happy—more than happy, with joy exploding from their faces—if they could find themselves in the fold, married for time and all eternity to someone they love. I know that joy is real, and it cannot possibly originate from the "cunningly devised fables" of one Joseph Smith. He was and is a prophet of God. I know it!

Ancient Connections

At the request of the Foundation for Ancient Research and Mormon Studies (FARMS), I finally managed to visit the curator of Egyptian antiquities at the Hermitage Museum of Art—a surprisingly young man—who kindly allowed us to photograph their two hypocephali, which resemble those in the Pearl of Great Price and date back to the first millennium B.C. One was papyrus encased in glass, the other made of wood. I was even invited to hold them in my hand, an act which would be unheard of anywhere in the West.

Walking through this central Romanov palace with the curator, I commented on its excessive opulence and said that, with all the royal edifices in the vicinity—we learn about one more every other week—there was probably never such a concentration of wealth and ostentation in the history of any other nation. He agreed, suggesting that in France, for example, the tokens of power and possession were more widely distributed from province to province, whereas during the Russian empire they were inordinately localized in a country whose territory was incomparably vast. This is another reason, I suppose, why the revolution occurred here and not somewhere else.

Nor does one walk central St. Petersburg's streets for long before noticing the plaques that adorn every third or fourth building, advertising what famous Russian had resided there for a time. Besides the obligatory Soviet general or politician, practically every noteworthy Russian

artist, composer, or writer from both this and the previous century is rec‐
ognized. St. Petersburg is another Florence, Vienna, and Paris—all in one.
It had comparable patronage, as its architecture still so vividly reminds
us, and remains, despite the ravages of socialism, one of the world's fore‐
most cultural centers. One of the few positive consequences of excessive
power and opulence.

Foundation Stone

This is a culture where, in their way, people have been extremely devout.
The Orthodox Church has played an important historical role in the na‐
tion's life, and religion has, over the centuries, offered solace to many a
Russian peasant who otherwise had a very bleak existence. For these
people, religion was, more than anything, I believe, a consolation for their
trials and oppression. There was a deep reverent feeling in those who wor‐
shiped during the Soviet era, even as there is now. These were mostly older
women who didn't have that much to lose for disclosing themselves as
believers. There also seems to have been a disposition on the part of the
Russian intelligentsia, more than with their counterparts in the West, to be
open to religion and, even if they weren't always aware of it, to want its
influence in their lives. Russian society still strikes one as virgin territory in
that regard.

Not Alone

From Sister Chartina Jarrett:

> My companion and I were traveling on a train from the metro in
> the Rzhevka area. For some reason, I've had such a difficult time talk‐
> ing to people in public vehicles. I guess it's the fear of men. But I feel
> very strongly about speaking to men in order to help build up the
> priesthood in St. Petersburg. And I just can't hold my testimony inside.
> The Spirit won't let me.
>
> So I started to speak to the men near me. One of them completely
> ignored me, and another was drunk. I felt worthless and wondered why
> I had bothered. Staring out the window, I threw a spiritual tantrum.
>
> "This is hard," I told myself. "I feel like giving up, quitting."
>
> "I know," the Spirit replied. The chastisement was so sweet my
> heart melted in understanding.

Then I thought of my Savior, who always knows who I am, where I am, and what I am doing. At that moment, I felt, more than anything else, an overwhelming gratitude for my Redeemer. I thought of his sacrifice and was filled with his love. I knew that he felt my discouragement and pain and would be there for me.

Curve Ball

A memorable Russian proverb suggests that life's passage is not as simple as crossing a "bare, flat field." Perhaps the most distressing experience so far has been to see three fine elders come down with mysterious maladies—chronic fatigue, clinical depression, kidney and back problems—that required them to leave the mission field. Though some suspected an attitude problem, I know it was otherwise. Out of our nearly ninety, I've yet to see a missionary who isn't trying her or his hardest to serve devotedly. And the sisters lead the pack. They are all so noble, so courageous, so steady for people their age.

Champions

From Elder Michael Morrison:

On Friday, January 28, the small township of Vyborg was shocked as a small group of Mormon missionaries took the town basketball championship before a crowd of several hundred. Our missionaries knew it would be tough as soon as Vyborg started the game with a three-pointer from the parking lot. But we quickly regained the lead and never looked back. Steady play and incredible defense led us to a 37–22 half-time lead. But even in the face of those odds, the Vyborg team would not give up.

In the second half, they came out with fire in their bellies and quickly closed the point spread. The home team crowd started to come alive, and it looked like trouble for the elders. But after a time-out to regroup, our missionaries unveiled their sweet steal! Every player played his role to the fullest: Elder Matthew Stepan, point guard and ball-handling machine; Elder Troy Peterson, Dennis Rodman on the boards; Elder Michael Hertig, commander and force in the middle; Elder Morrison, swat team with six blocked shots; Elder Kenneth Dinkel, defense like Michael Cooper; and Elders Brendan Parker and John Rather coming off the bench with strong contributions. Elder Matthew Scoll was the man in the clutch. With a three-pointer and a twenty-foot jumper late in the game, he put the butter in the fridge and ended any hopes of a last-minute Vyborg comeback. With great passes and a stall offense, we held on to take the championship with a 60–52 win.

But my message isn't just about basketball. I'd like to suggest what we can do when Satan is making a comeback. Take a time-out and regroup. Read the scriptures and say a prayer. Don't wait for it to happen. Forget about President Rogers's "No Slam Dunk" rule and stuff one—Two-Hands-behind-the-Head-Double-Pump-Chocolate-Thunder—right over Satan!

Something Else

During the monthly firesides with investigators, certain otherwise promising and intelligent candidates for baptism raise rather idiosyncratic objections to our message. They say, "The Book of Mormon teaches the traditional doctrine of the Trinity" or "God is love and ordinances don't matter." Or they have their own private agenda: "I'm so impressed with your family-centeredness. Please find me a sponsor so that I can direct an orphanage and help the destitute learn these principles." This response reminds me of nothing so much as the anecdote, told in Dostoevsky's novel *The Idiot:* "I was talking to an atheist the other day, who gave me all these reasons why God does not exist. But he was really talking about something else."

Healer

All things here seem cyclical and recurring. The impasse with Elder X, who, during that first round of missionary interviews, seemed to take umbrage when I rejected his suggestions, has been quite unexpectedly resolved. Time is a great healer in personal as in public affairs—if one waits long enough, the discord is diffused. Nothing stays the same forever but moves onto its opposite.

Feminist Paradox

Something that seems almost irrelevant here is the ongoing controversy back home regarding women's rights, abortion, and so forth. Women in Russia are generally far more abused by men—particularly in marriage—to the point that relatively few marriages remain intact. The State imposition of abortion, until recently the sole means of control over family size, also strikes many here as an indisputable evil and a further form of abuse.

In many cases, marriage in Russia seems only to insure that partners will be less inclined to move serially on to others, strewing their path with neglected dependents and ending their lives in utter loneliness. Like the putting on of clothes, marriage is seen as another needful, if at times rather artificial, custom. In fact, many Russian women do not care to have a man in the house any more—the man being too often an adult child that the woman must clean up after and cook for and that would in most cases drunkenly abuse her. Russian women want, ideally, to have one child and some close female friends, but not necessarily a husband. Only at this point do their protests begin to reflect those of some feminists in the West.

Opposition in All Things

I'm still learning, although not quickly enough, that in this position you can't just arbitrarily say yes to people. They come at you from all directions with their special pleas. You're in no position to dispute their need, yet you have to tell them that, on principle, you cannot lend them the Church van or help them emigrate. You have to be careful not to alienate them because you also personify the Church to them. And it's hard to always keep that in mind. Whenever anyone I don't know calls me for an appointment without explaining the reason, I can be sure she or he is going to present me with some scheme involving money. Luckily, I can refer the party back to President Efimov and the local leaders for the funds our leaders in Frankfurt and I can authorize only upon our local leaders' recommendation. If the petitioners insist that it's a life-and-death matter and they must have aid immediately, it's most likely a deception.

Other Forces

Events this week have led me to a keen realization. Though I may be in charge here and am expected to hold out a sense of vision to others—which I try to do—I am in less control of what transpires in others' lives or of what is accomplished organizationally than in any enterprise in which I was ever engaged. But that is exactly as it should be. Other forces than our own take over, including everyone's free will and their need to be challenged and tested and sometimes buffeted before things go smoothly. Involvement in the Church unavoidably provides that opportunity. It is a great laboratory for the development of souls, if over a lifetime one allows it to serve that purpose.

Courtesy Gail Halvorsen

Hard working women, like this one, are often the backbone of the Russian family and society. In addition to their child-rearing responsibilities, many women will also work two or three jobs in order to provide sufficient sustenance for their family.

Raised Eyebrows

I tried to rescue three elders who, after a half year, seemed totally incapable of teaching even a first discussion. We decided to hold a month-long refresher course for them. To give it a certain extra weight, I titled it, offhandedly, our own "School of the Prophets." As might have been expected, one of them wrote to his parents, then on a service mission at the Church Office Building. Shortly after, we received a concerned inquiry from members of the Quorum of the Twelve: What was I doing reinstituting the School of the Prophets? I could only hope they had not also heard—out of context—about my dabbling with Egyptian hypocephali at the Hermitage.

Beatific

At our last district leadership meeting, a beautiful thing occurred concerning the difference of opinion between two leaders—one a branch president, the other his district president. The branch president had just invited others interested to join him and the members of his branch to meet on Sunday afternoon at the Russian Museum for a lecture by a specialist on the religious paintings there. The district president warned about violating the Sabbath. Because each was concerned about not offending the other, neither insisted that the other was totally in the wrong. It was a moment of grace. One could have wished that we would always address or regard each other, even at home, with such basic respect and concern for the other's feelings.

Rich Encounters: Spring 1994

Rude Awakening

On an early spring day, Merriam and our daughter Mary noticed what proved to be a man's fur-wrapped and *shapka*-hooded corpse floating in the Moika Canal, which fronts the mission home. (Each spring hundreds of people fall through the Neva River ice, which one can walk across in very cold weather. Other fatalities are suicides or are dumped there by their criminal assailants.) Merriam at first thought it must be something else, but Mary insisted, "Mom, you're in denial!" When Mary next saw her brother Will, she related to him the unsavory encounter, only to be topped by "I've seen at least three corpses since being here—and close enough to know how bad they smell!"

This Too Shall Pass

Every two months since we have been here, there has been a crisis: the pending legislation against foreign religious entities, Yeltsin's showdown with the parliament in Moscow, and now the more recent elections which were so overwhelmingly supportive of Vladimir Zhirinovsky. By now I am so inured to such crises that I am fairly—perhaps too much so—complacent about what might happen next. One thing is sure: nothing will stay quite the same for very long, but whatever does come next "shall also pass." It seems more like a kaleidoscope that gets periodically shaken and rearranged, affording each time a different and always interesting new landscape.

Joseph and Judah

Perhaps nowhere so much as in Russia do we manage to reach and convert Jews. Russian Jews, disabused of their fathers' tradition by Soviet indoctrination, have remained Jews nonetheless, with all their wonderful traits and special gifts. [Two such were serving as branch presidents when we left the mission.]

In the Lord's Hands

From Elder Rick Davis:

> Elder Matthew Lamont and I stood at the front doors of the metro station. The people we were contacting were mostly hurrying to work. However, one young man, dressed in the typical "Mafia" leather jacket and Italian shoes, stopped for us. Then he proceeded to display a little red book covered with coffee stains, which, it turns out, was a kind of badge. He said he intended to arrest us as American spies. Elder Lamont, who had been in Russia for only two months, watched the exchange of words between myself and the alleged cop with growing concern. I was sure the badge was a fake and that he wanted to rob us.

> As we continued to argue, a second and then a third voice sounded behind us. All at once, I felt the barrel of a pistol against my back. We were in big trouble. My companion and I looked at each other and silently prayed, putting the whole situation in Father's hands. We then agreed to our captors' demands. It turned out that they were indeed the police. We were briefly arrested, interrogated, searched, and then released.

> What we learned from the incident was that, once we put the situation in the Lord's hands, our fear vanished, and by no longer resisting or contending, we were finally led out of danger.

Amazing "Coincidences"

In 1991 a young girl from Kirgizstan approached a professor who, with his LDS students, had been touring Petersburg and was on the way to a Sunday service. She asked the professor to help her find the branch of the church that coincidentally they were also looking for. She had halfheartedly agreed to attend church at the urging of people associated with the Tabernacle Choir, whose concert she had attended during its tour of Russia the week before. However, she had silently told God that if she did not find where the Church was meeting her obligation to look further would be satisfied. Just three years later, as she was set apart to serve a mission in Moscow, Sister Kalambubu Turgunalievna Murzakulova reminded the professor, now her mission president, where they had first met.

Again in 1990, a young man, noticing two missionaries in a subway car, had the strong urge to speak to them, but the missionaries did not approach him. Two years later, he and his family were tracted out by another pair of messengers. He attests to the "light" that radiated from them as they entered his apartment. Vladimir Astafev now presides over St. Petersburg's Moskovsky Branch.

Another young man and his family attest to the similar presence they felt when the missionaries came to them. Sergey Smelov is now president of the branch in the St. Petersburg suburb Kolpino.

In 1991 a young woman, an accomplished pianist, was taking a train to the Ukraine to recover from the shock of her brother's untimely death. Before the woman boarded, her mother noticed there were only men on the train and advised her daughter to dispose of her ticket and go another time. Then a young American, a returned missionary who had served in another country but was then touring Russia, happened to approach them. He told them he had been prompted in a dream the night before to offer his services to someone that day, and in halting Russian, he offered his protection. For some reason, they trusted him. Learning during the trip about his religious background, the young woman decided to look up the Church after returning home. Asking some young people, who proved to be Baptists, for directions, she was told to beware of the Mormons, who would shout at her and compel her to stay with them. Remembering the young man, she disbelieved them and went on her way. Jana Orno-Orlova is now our mission's music director and shouts at us to stay in tune!

For several years, a man had taken special notice of one of the principal supervisors at his large workplace. The supervisor, he says, stood out for him because of his honesty and his concern for others. After joining the Church, the first man was both amazed and delighted to discover this exceptionally fine supervisor, Vyacheslav Efimov, was his district president. [Later Efimov became the first Russian mission president to serve in Russia.]

In 1993 a missionary was unexpectedly impelled to cross a busy street and speak to a family he had noticed at a considerable distance. The husband, Anatoly Sitonin, then considered himself an atheist, but he and his wife were baptized soon after taking the missionary lessons. Six months later, he served as a branch president and shortly after replaced Vyacheslav Efimov as president of St. Petersburg's East District. He later became a counselor in the mission presidency.

Speaking recently with another of our strong district presidents, I learned that, during the three years *before* he and his family encountered the missionaries, he had not only given up coffee and tea but also had begun to hold his own family home evening. He had also moved from the stance of a convinced atheist to debating matters of faith within himself (the first year), then to submitting to the inner "voice" that argued for faith (the second year), and finally to recognizing that "voice" as indeed the voice of God (the third year). While attending the temple a year after their conversion, he immediately recognized that same familiar "voice." He

Elders proselytizing at a metro station. Missionaries often sang hymns at metro stations to attract attention and draw crowds—one of the more creative ways of introducing people to the gospel. *Front row, from left:* Kyle Hill, Ryan Neumann, Brendan Parker, Andrew Eversole. *Back row, from left:* Kenneth Dinkel, John Valentine, and Joshua Gardner.

heard it again when he began to read the Doctrine and Covenants for the first time.

After a fresh falling-out with his senior companion, a young, tender-hearted missionary began to cry as he approached a man on the street. The man responded by embracing and consoling the missionary but did not agree to take a Book of Mormon or meet with him. The next day while tracting, the missionaries reencountered the same man, who remembered the tender-hearted elder and was moved by what had earlier transpired between them. The man invited them in and began receiving the discussions.

While riding in a bus a few weeks ago to the farewell sacrament service featuring a local sister missionary called to Moscow, I noticed a young man and an older lady enter the vehicle. Their backs were turned, and through the crowd I could not see them well. But something about the young man—not just the suit and tie he wore, but his deference to the woman, presumably his mother—made me regret that he was not one of us or one of our missionaries, whom he so resembled. It was an impression I don't usually have when I'm in a crowd of strangers. I asked myself what it would take to reach people like this young man. One could even assume, given their dress and bearing, that the young man and his mother were going to a church service of one kind or another. Russians don't ordinarily dress that well or that formally, particularly on Sunday.

But why not to our service? I felt I should approach them and invite them to investigate the Church. But before I had a chance to, the young man turned in my direction—and, behold, it was the brother of our sister missionary, himself a member who had joined after participating in our mission play a year earlier. During the sacrament meeting, he spoke and announced his desire to serve a mission, too. In the aftermath, I asked myself what about him already stood out so? (I think I know.) And I chided myself: more is happening "out there" than we are often aware. The appeal of and need for the restored gospel, as well as its amazing comprehensiveness, are truly universal. If that were not so, we could not reach people like that young man, his mother, and his sister, and we would have long ago returned home. [Aleksandr Nepomnyashchy has since then also served a Russian-speaking mission and is now president of the same branch to which I traveled on that memorable Sunday.]

A Glimpse of Heaven

In the company of visiting General Authorities, we recently entered a rented auditorium for a combined missionary zone conference. There they stood in a long, unbroken line along two walls and in front of the stage, waiting to greet us—our ninety or so angel missionaries. At the sight of them, I literally wept with love and admiration. Is that what it's like—our reception by loved ones on the other side? What more could one ever ask or hope for?

Looking Good

If average parents want to impress their children, they should just send them on a mission. From my daughter Mary's journal:

> Very often the head of a Russian home is either the mother or the *babushka* [grandma]. In many cases, the only thing a father contributes

to his family are his genes, leaving the rest of the work to his wife if he sticks around at all.

I remember attending a Russian Relief Society meeting one Sunday where most of the sisters were single. The lesson dealt with supporting the priesthood holder as head of the household. The sisters had a hard time relating to such a far-fetched idea. Some of the *babushkas* even laughed out loud at the thought of a man working to support his family and then coming home to help his wife raise his children. To me, that was just an every day aspect of life—one I hadn't given much thought to. There was one incident, however, that made me think twice about my family, especially my father.

One day I was at a metro station, waiting for a friend. Just in front of me, I noticed a man, bent over on his hands and knees. It was an all-too-familiar scene. "He's drunk and he's throwing up," I thought. I was right about the first part, but as I got closer, I realized he wasn't vomiting. He just couldn't keep his balance, and that's why he was on the floor. Each time he tried to get up, he got so dizzy

Courtesy Andrew Eversole

Planning transfers. President Rogers and his missionary assistants, Elders Andrew Eversole and John Valentine, carefully prayed about and considered each missionary's current companion and city. A particular city and companion can greatly influence a missionary's attitude.

that after a couple of steps he stumbled and fell back down. As I watched him, I was reminded of the helpless feeling I've experienced just before passing out.

People were yelling at the man to get out of their way. He made one more attempt to walk but instead fell this time, head first, smack on the cement. I was close enough to hear the sound his head made and could see the pained look on his face. Then I realized with horror that if he had gone a couple of feet farther, he'd have stumbled onto the tracks of the metro. I wanted to cry. I wanted to do something to help this man I didn't even know. But my friend showed up and was already ten feet ahead, ready to board our train. So I ran to catch up to him and left the man in his helpless condition.

I don't know why this scene has affected me so much. I've witnessed others like it, but I couldn't get it out of my mind. I found myself thinking about it the rest of the day, and as I did, something else came to my mind: that man is probably someone's father. Then I thought, "What if he were my father? What if my father got so drunk he couldn't stand up and people were yelling at him to get out of their way?" I felt so grateful to have a father who is hardworking and able to support and care for his family. A lot of people don't have that, and not just in Russia.

Reasoning Together

I've heard somewhere that transfers—reassigning missionary companionships—is my most important task and one that no one else can do. While I respect that principle, I also know that our transfers would often be far less "right" or inspired if I did not closely consult with my missionary assistants. Besides excellent judgment, they so often have information and insight about other missionaries to which I am not privy. On more than one occasion, they've persuaded me to see things differently, and I don't consider that in any way a default of my own inspiration. In fact, my willingness to *counsel* seriously with my counselors [as, later, both President Howard W. Hunter and Elder M. Russell Ballard would urge] strikes me as a most inspired initiative. The scriptural admonition "Let us reason together" (D&C 50:10) keeps coming to mind. What, in fact, would a mission president do without such able, inspired assistants?

Tempted

Some of our most able members are finding ways to emigrate, deceptively traveling abroad on tourist visas, then not returning. The U.S. consulate now suspects Latter-day Saint Russians and does not much trust them.

Impediments to Missionary Work

There seem to be five general causes of discouragement and depression in missionaries:

1. *Physical or emotional impairments.* If these persist, little can be done besides sending the missionary home early.

2. *Companion incompatibility.* I usually try to band-aid companion problems with a quick transfer, assuming that missionaries face enough other challenges. If this issue doesn't go away after multiple transfers, it begins to resemble a form of emotional impairment, which is then terribly frustrating for all concerned.

3. *Initial adjustment.* Missionaries must adjust to a new language, culture, taxing routine, and the need to study harder than they usually ever did as college freshmen. In addition, they face recurring rejection by most of those they speak to. This adjustment can last as long as half a year. The only solution is to tough it out until things change for the better—and most of them eventually do, in some cases miraculously.

4. *Burnout before the end.* Here again seeming miracles are often called for and sometimes occur—complete rejuvenation, flame from cold ashes.

5. *A sense of personal unworthiness* (mostly concerning offenses on the lower end of the scale). I tend to underplay this concern where there is still a strong resolve, telling missionaries that even though we are imperfect vessels we are needed and useful. Missionaries should defer their concern about worthiness, which in some areas may take a long time to resolve—even beyond their mission—and meanwhile keep working (which is its own cure for many an ill and temptation). As, with a twinkle in his eye, President Boyd K. Packer declared to assembled mission presidents and wives in Frankfurt after first addressing us during a morning-long session, "I pronounce you good enough." The Lord has invested too heavily in his emissaries not to stand by them, despite their imperfections.

Discouragement itself—whatever its cause—strikes me as the worst impediment of all, and maybe it helps to tell the missionaries so, as I do quite regularly.

"Chunks" of Reality

I find solace in the words of one of our very sensitive missionaries and a former student of mine, Elder Jeffery Flint:

> On a dark and cold Russian winter's evening (at 5 P.M.), Elder Hunter and I were crossing a street at the intersection of Prospekt Slavy and Budapeshtskaya. As we roamed with the herd towards the other side, a boy about ten years old came streaming between us, racing for the other curb. No sooner had we seen him than we heard his mother's voice calling after him with a riveting sense of distress. He halted, and along the path of his next intended footstep whirled a car that none of us had seen. The child stood, wide-eyed at the vivid fact that he doubtless would have died from the impact of the recklessly speeding car. Everyone showed the strain of horror, then relief, realizing what should have happened but did not.
>
> That wasn't our only brush that day with what seemed an imminent death. On the same street a kilometer farther, outside a market known to most missionaries in our area, we came upon a man writhing on the ground, his face turning red, then purple and then white. Already a loose crowd had formed around him. Since he was no more than thirty, I couldn't understand what was wrong with him. It couldn't be a heart attack, I thought. As I tried to recall how to apply CPR, two men jumped in to try to help him. The man twisted and turned some more and then became deathly limp. I thought he had died in front of me, and I felt a desire to grab him and squeeze the life back into him. I almost expected to catch a glimpse of his spirit leaving his body. But the man didn't die. It was an epileptic seizure, possibly complicated by his tongue blocking the wind passage.
>
> I'll never forget that moment as, helplessly, we watched him fade from us. It was a chunk of reality that instantaneously caused the flashy cars and the leather coats that dotted the market to seem idiotic and needless, the furs and cosmetics of the stylish shoppers quite pointless. Together with the saving call of the mother's voice, it served to remind me of who we really are and what we are all here for. It made me want to shun life's masquerade and simply live, unafraid of others' opinions and unashamed before God, giving those who don't understand an explanation, but not a justification, to prioritize my life according to God's will, knowing that when the Moment comes, it will be his Son's voice calling us from the path of nonnegotiable death—his voice calling our name so that, hopefully, we will recognize it in time.

Overwhelming

Each year on March 8, Russians observe Women's Day—a holiday little known in the West. On this one day, far more than at other times, men pay special attention to the women in their lives, including female colleagues and associates in the work place. Merriam was completely overwhelmed when on that date one of the branch presidents from a suburb south of St. Petersburg appeared at the mission home door, bouquet in hand. Besides his own wife, he'd thought to honor the "mission mother." [At Easter, a sister came a similar distance with newly budded pussy willows. Such thoughtful gestures and the expenditure they represent in time and effort are not uncommon among our very loving members.]

Unique

One thing is crystal clear—what in terms of Christ's Atonement distinguishes the Church from all others. It is our understanding of the essential nature of covenants, beginning with baptism. Any denomination that baptizes infants—as with Orthodoxy and Catholicism—immediately nullifies the force of the covenantal relationship through baptism. And any denomination that, even after baptizing adults by immersion, presupposes that one is thereby automatically saved, similarly ignores or fails to understand that same covenantal relationship. Both practices make the application of religion to life far less engaging.

Another important distinction, for which we are regarded as blasphemers, is the restored gospel's vision of human destiny in terms of potential perfection and deification. But we didn't think this concept up to aggrandize ourselves. It's the truly amazing good news that God himself revealed to a latter-day prophet. And it's intended for all God's children. So why should it make us feel uncomfortable or believe that we need apologize for declaring it? This same principle—that human beings are divine heirs—also profoundly relates the doctrine of covenants to the Atonement. As Joseph Smith would say, it either tastes good to you, or it doesn't. One thing is sure, no one else teaches these concepts. If they are as fundamental and true as we believe, then that alone makes the Church unique and enforces its claim to being a part of Christ's one true kingdom. The Church both promises and requires so much more than any other enterprise I know.

Attributes

What characterizes those who distinctively and positively contribute to the kingdom as opposed to those who just go along for the ride (recognizing that there is a little of both in each of us)?

- Generosity and caring about others, with the inclination to be inconvenienced and to sacrifice in their behalf—to be more a giver than a taker (a first but basic step in sufficiently loving others).

- Common sense and moderation, avoiding the irrationality and fanaticism that too often beset us.

Courtesy John Bradshaw

Kingdom builders: Vyborg missionaries after a zone conference. Mission presidents meet with their missionaries monthly to provide instruction and training. These conferences are essential in establishing camaraderie among missionaries and their leaders as well as in enhancing missionaries' knowledge of the gospel and missionary skills. *From left:* Traver Maxwell, Christian Kaelin, Brian Evans, Joseph Everett, Aaron Harrison, Stewart Peay, President and Sister Rogers, Paul Tucker, John Bradshaw, David Koch, and Matthew Goodrich.

- Surrendering of one's will and idiosyncratic preferences to the Lord's will, particularly in the context of his Church (which also means complying with the expectations of those we consider his mouthpieces). This characteristic requires meekness and humility.
- Constancy and reliability in exercising the three foregoing, without which we can readily undo the benefit of what we may have accomplished in applying them.

Special Guest

From Mary's journal:

> Last week I went to an institute class in a member's home where there were only three class members in attendance. I felt guilty for not taking an institute or religion class last semester back home. It's so easy and available. You can choose from many different classes and teachers and be literally surrounded by people your own age who are doing the same thing. But the Spirit was very strong in the class I attended here in Russia. The teacher, Sister Mints, told us afterward, "There are four of you here, not three, because the Holy Ghost is also with us."

Really True

I recall the first time we and other mission presidents and wives met for a daylong orientation. We were addressed by Missionary Department personnel, then at day's end by Elder Richard Scott, who had just flown in from South America and came directly to us from the airport. As we were breaking up but still within earshot, he spoke with one of the wives. I heard him remark, with the same simple, soft-spoken intensity with which he'd addressed us, "It's really true." It was a testimony reminiscent of Joseph Smith's, when he declared, "He lives! For we saw him" (D&C 76:22–23).

Quick Reply

Again from Elder Jeffery Flint:

> Elder Charles G. Hunter III and I were on our way out when the phone rang. It was Sister Natasha, a recently reactivated member and mother of a great thirteen-year-old son. In an unusually panicked voice, she told us that Kirill should have returned from school two

hours ago. She was worried that a group of older boys who only last week had tried to extort protection money might have ambushed him after school because of his and her refusal to pay. She asked us to help.

I was dumbfounded and felt a little threatened by her request. Even if we located his school, what could we do two hours late? Then a previous experience occured to me. We had offered to help a member whose life was reeling with complications. Her simple, trusting response had been, "Just pray for me."

Elder Hunter and I knelt to give one of those prayers. I wished I could feel such sincerity every day. As my companion expressed our words of hope, the phone rang. It was Natasha: Kirill had called her from a friend's house. Everything was all right. Setting down the phone, I assumed that Elder Hunter already sensed Natasha's good news and asked him to keep praying, assuming he would now express our thanksgiving. As he continued to plead for Kirill's safety, I smiled and said, "Have faith. That was Sister Natasha. Everything's okay." Prayers and answers. Short, sweet, and to the point.

Bless Us All

It increasingly dawns on me that about the best thing any of us can do is be kind and considerate toward everyone. One of the worst things I could ever do in this calling is to exempt anyone whatsoever from that kind of attention by dismissing or dealing with him or her indifferently or unfeelingly. Yet how often have I probably done so, even if unintentionally. It's the sentiment of the hero Alexander's remarkable prayer in Andrey Tarkovsky's last and spiritually culminating film, *Sacrifice*:

> Our Father, who art in Heaven. . . . Deliver us in this terrible time. . . . All those who love Thee and believe in Thee. All those who do not believe in Thee because they are blind. Those who haven't given Thee a thought simply because they haven't yet been truly miserable. All those who in this hour have lost their hope, their future, their lives and the opportunity to surrender to Thy will.

So I regularly pray for others, as well as for the members, missionaries, and investigators.

Year Two

Summer 1994
to
Spring 1995

True Disciples: Summer 1994

Household of Saints

A while back, I attended the retrospective exhibition of propagandistic art on display at the Russian Museum, just ten minutes' walk from our headquarters. The exhibit is unabashedly titled *Agitatsiya za schaste* (*Agitation for Happiness*), an appropriate enough description of what we, too, are undertaking. It evokes the communality and fellowship—as much traditionally Russian as Soviet—that I came to identify with the Russia I first visited in 1958, five years after Stalin's death.

Russians of my generation stood in the museum with me. Patriotic anthems from the period wafted around us. As we viewed the mammoth, heroic group portraits of beaming young athletes, peasants, and laborers, we were nostalgically transported back to those times, the only life these older Russians had known until lately. Those were times when supposedly streets were safe, bread and housing were available to all, a sense of communal solidarity and existential purpose was reinforced daily, and everyone was ruddily healthy and celestially happy (at least so depicted).

Though aware of how Russians had been so cruelly manipulated, we nevertheless sensed a certain good faith, wholesomeness, and camaraderie that went with their high purpose, now utterly lost. As best I can see, there are only two things on hand to profoundly replace it: the spiritual idealism and communal involvement that the Church offers these people—in spades.

There are interesting parallels between social interaction in the Church and the earlier experience of the Russians in peasant communes in the Soviet period—the sense of accountability and concern for one another's temporal and moral (spiritual) well-being. In fact, I find that this same feeling of fellowship and this service mindedness are far more the case with LDS congregations than with most others, including Orthodoxy itself. It's this affinity that I have always felt would make the Church so appealing to Russians. And I think the Church does have that appeal for any person who gives it a chance. The Church isn't therefore so utterly foreign to those who first encounter it.

But I have also discovered in many a tendency to be indifferent to the fate and welfare of strangers. Russians are very supportive of their immediate family group, their significant others, and their very small circle of close friends. (This is an endearing trait. In the West, we don't, on the whole, have close friends who mean as much to us as they do to Russians.) But

Courtesy Morgan Magleby

Building solidarity. Elders Bret Fund and Robert Wirthlin (*front center, left to right*) partici-pate in a cookie-eating contest with the Piskaryovsky Branch. Missionaries are encouraged to attend ward activities. Their participation strengthens members' and promotes goodwill among all concerned.

Russians can walk by a corpse on the street or encounter someone in extreme agony and not pay any attention if they don't know the person. When they join the Church, they have to expand their circle to include those they don't already know or care much about, and that can be a con-siderable challenge.

Celestial Contact

From Elder Kevin Hathaway:

> For several days in a row, my companion and I had spent our mornings street contacting. We would always cross the soccer field in front of our apartment, ride the bus a few blocks, and then contact on the streets next to the metro.

On this particular morning, however, we decided that, instead of crossing the soccer field, we would take a different route along the edge of the building in order to avoid the heat of the sun. As we emerged from behind the building onto an unfamiliar street, we saw a tall, muscular man and his petite wife pushing a baby carriage in our direction. As missionaries, we'd been challenged to speak to someone within three minutes of leaving our apartments. On this morning, it was my turn to make the first contact, so I approached the large man with the respect and caution his immense size demanded.

He was surprisingly polite and agreed to listen to my message. He told us his name was Aleksandr Tomak. For the next few minutes, he listened intently as I introduced myself and told him a little bit about the Church. When I removed a Book of Mormon from my bag to show him, his eyes immediately widened and he ceased looking at me. For the rest of our conversation, his gaze was focused on that Book of Mormon. He agreed to meet with us the next day, and when I gave him the book, he cradled it gently in his hands as if it were a small child.

When we arrived the next day to teach Aleksandr the first discussion, he had already read fifteen chapters in the Book of Mormon. It took several minutes to answer all his questions before we could begin to teach him the discussion. Over the next month, I was amazed to see him grow. He attended church every week and continued reading the Book of Mormon. I could soon see the sparkle of a testimony in his eyes.

Only one obstacle stood between Aleksandr and baptism. He loved to smoke. He told me later that after weeks of struggling with that habit, he finally approached the Lord in prayer. He told the Lord how grateful he was for the Church and the Book of Mormon. He expressed his burning desire to be baptized and then asked the Lord to help him quit smoking. As he opened his eyes, they immediately came to rest on a pack of cigarettes. He removed one of them and looked at it. Suddenly he realized that his physical craving to smoke had disappeared. The cigarette in his hand did not even appeal to him. In fact, it was repulsive. He tossed the whole pack over his balcony railing and walked back into his apartment. From that moment, Aleksandr has never experienced the craving for a cigarette!

I baptized Aleksandr on August 6. The ordinance was performed in a lake not far from his home. As he came up out of the water, his face shone with light. My emotions grew tender as he immersed me in a giant bear hug. I felt like I'd been preparing for that moment for nineteen years.

Later, Aleksandr told me that on the morning we first met, he and his wife had both "just turned down that unfamiliar street for no particular reason." I know without a doubt, as does Aleksandr, that there was a reason why we both decided to take different streets that morning. It had nothing to do with chance or the heat of the day. The Lord needed Aleksandr and his family.

[Brother Tomak was soon called as a branch president and faithfully served in that capacity for several months. During that time, he also baptized his wife, Yulya. Today he is the president of St. Petersburg's largest district. He continues to be an example of faith and obedience to those he serves.]

No One an Island

I often experience a state of being that isn't anything I so much feel as something I become one with when I am fully in accord and effortlessly attentive. It affords a state of transcendent, transpersonal calm, similar to the awed detachment relished after climbing a mountain, while standing on the rim of the Grand Canyon or the bottom of Zion Canyon, and when staring at a campfire or at ocean breakers. On such occasions, I am para-doxically reminded both of my minuteness and of my intrinsic belonging to and participation in the natural, universal order.

But where have I experienced it most keenly and most often? In every missionary testimony meeting I have ever attended (including three years of them at the Missionary Training Center and two and a half years in Germany decades ago). Also wherever the Saints testify in simple, candid, but utterly earnest fashion—which, in my experience, they most often do.

He Qualifies

From Mary's journal:

> When I visited the sisters in Vyborg, I had a special experience. As we approached the building where the meetings are held, Sister Myers asked me out of the blue if I would like to bear my testimony in sacrament meeting. "You mean, bear it in English, and you translate?" I naively asked. "No," she said, *"po-russki"* ["in Russian"]. She knew I'd studied a little bit of Russian. "Little" is an overstatement. Her request left me terrified. I'm very intimidated about speaking what few Russian phrases I know, especially in front of native speakers, but for some rea-son I agreed to do it.

> I was fortunate to skim through a hymn book and a paper my mom had given me the day before with useful phrases for prayers. During the beginning of the meeting, I referred to these sources and

frantically tried to scribble down what I was going to say. I also found a scripture I could read. Toward the end of the meeting, the branch president announced, "We will now hear from Mary Rogers—President Rogers's daughter." (As if I were famous or something.) I got up and smiled to hide my fear.

I think what happened next was a miracle. No, I didn't preach a perfect sermon with the gift of tongues. But I was able to bear my humble testimony in Russian, and the congregation were able to understand me. When I finished, I felt the Spirit so strongly that I was shaking after I sat down. I know I couldn't have spoken like that without the help of my Heavenly Father and was extremely grateful. I know I wasn't by myself when I stood before that congregation.

Role Model

We were recently invited by one of our branch presidents, Viktor Yakovlev, to the dacha he built with his father and brother. While there, we experienced a Russian *banya* (hot steam sauna) and were then served a simple meal made up entirely of the products from his dacha garden—boiled potatoes, tomato preserves, fresh cabbage, and apples—taken from the root cellar he had also constructed.

What made the experience particularly profound was that this man, though a professor and an engineer, hasn't been paid for half a year. For the very survival of his family, he needs what he grows. Hospitable as ever and in my experience never inclined to ask for a handout or special help, he just happens to be one of the longest-standing branch presidents in St. Petersburg. He also testifies that two summers ago he worked in his garden only one Sunday and came up with a miserable crop. This year he vowed to avoid Sunday gardening altogether and produced a bumper harvest. The bounty testifies to him of the principle of Sabbath keeping. His example testifies to us of that and much more.

Celestial Presence

The words of three members—two of them now branch presidents—stand out for me. Each has mentioned the noticeable "feeling" or "light" that the missionaries brought on their first visit. That light is what most impelled these members to receive the lessons and to so dedicatedly and, in some respects, radically change their lives. One of them, a young father and a particularly angelic person, even thanked the other branch presidents at our latest leadership session for the love he felt in their presence. What wonderfully simple, innocent recognition of goodness and fellow feeling. Could any gift be greater than the open acknowledgment of what really matters most?

Latter-day Almas

In the Doctrine and Covenants, the Lord rebukes his missionaries for failing to "open their mouths" (D&C 60:2). Truly, that is what they are sent out to do. Elder X, who at the outset so worried me, and an elder from Idaho disposed to broadcast his radical political views have emerged as two

of our most sterling examples of the fearlessness and dedication the Lord expects from us all. Outstanding priesthood leaders have emerged from among these missionaries' investigators, while the small group originally shepherded by the Idaho elder has become one of our strongest units. Its members still adore his memory.

A third elder with the same qualities was with us for only six weeks before moving on to the Ukraine, to which he was originally assigned. He'd joined the Church at age twenty-three just before graduating from an eastern Ivy League institution. Part of his attraction to the Church was his direct descent from an earlier president of the Church, despite intervening generations

Courtesy Wendy Bingham Stepan

Angelic refrain. Sister Melissa Myers (Jorgensen), an accomplished harpist, played her instrument at concerts and in public parks, attracting large crowds and more than one eventual convert.

of inactivity. This elder noticeably radiates a special maturity and sense of total conversion. He is blessed for this, as are all who encounter him.

By contrast, there are some (fortunately, I'm aware of only a few) who exceedingly fear proselytizing and, when they consent to go through the motions, avoid as much as possible approaching strangers with their message. One very lovable and charismatic elder confessed to me as he was about to return home that he essentially had never approached a single Russian with our message during the entire twenty-two months of his mission. I know that every morning all missionaries fear to some degree facing the unknown. Some of the strongest have told me so. And that's what makes them so heroic. I hope and pray that those who falter and so agonizingly resist contacting nevertheless manage somehow to bless others' lives, including their own.

Zion Prospers

We received authorization yesterday to divide the two Church districts that were formed in St. Petersburg in September just last year. We will shortly have a total of four, in addition to the one in Vyborg. It's a significant moment in the ongoing growth of the Church here. It will lighten the burden of our current district presidents, enabling each of the four new ones to operate within a more confined geographical area and to concentrate on fewer units. We nevertheless hope to add new embryo-branches (called "groups") as the missionary force gradually increases in the fall. (We now have around 90 missionaries but were recently authorized to have a larger complement of 126.) When we came here a year ago, the mission had only one district and eleven branches. Now there are nineteen branches and four groups. With additional missionaries, we will be able to divide as many as four of the existing branches and add as many as eight new groups, mostly in the suburbs to the north and south.

Trade-Off

In Vyborg we are trying to find more appealing places to meet in—necessarily at greater expense. The buildings the members have used till now are dark, dingy caverns, as are a number in St. Petersburg. But this drawback doesn't seem to impede the spirit of those who find their way there, so maybe more impressive edifices are a kind of trade-off.

However, I'm now more reconciled than I was earlier to the opulence of our new mission home and office. They truly seem to make the Church more respectable in the members' eyes. Earlier I felt we were enjoying a splendor to which even Merriam and I were unaccustomed. The contrast is so striking here between third-world squalor, for which most people have to settle, and the sated materialistic culture of the West. One is hard put to choose between them. Both are fairly debilitating; neither very fulfilling.

Lots of Fun

From Mary's journal:

> After tracting for a day with the sisters in Vyborg, I stayed that night at their apartment, but none of us slept too well. We were wakened by loud talk and then yelling from outdoors. I just thought it was people who had stayed up late because of the white nights [the long nights in midsummer when the sun barely sets]. But then I heard a woman scream, and I jumped out of bed to see what was going on. Sister Bingham was already up and looking out the window. She told us that the people were all drunk, and there was going to be a fight. I looked out the window too (the sisters live on the fifth floor) and saw about five or six men and one woman, all staggering around on the street below. Several men were ganging up on one man, who was apparently the woman's boyfriend.
>
> As the other men approached him, his girlfriend would jump in front of him and start screaming not to touch him but to leave him alone because he was drunk. "Don't listen to him," she pled. "He's drunk and doesn't know what he's talking about!" He'd apparently been egging the others on. The woman sobbed hysterically the whole time. Luckily, before anything more happened, a police car pulled up to settle things, so we went back to bed. But I could still hear the woman screaming as hysterically as ever. Then Sister Bingham said something that basically sums up how I felt: "I will never know why people think that drinking is so much fun."

Pure Motives

One thing accounts, I believe, for the especially strong, devoted members the Church tends to attract here (despite the inevitable backsliding and inactivity, which are the other side of the coin). So much is required that people will simply *not* join or stay active without a personal witness that is fairly all consuming. Just think of what it takes for them to give up drinking tea.

Gift of Tongues

Merriam has worked hard on the language. It hasn't come easy, and it rarely does for folks our age. Almost every Sunday now, she bears her testimony. She also gives a short talk at every conference—all in Russian. She's motivated, more than ever, to keep studying the language after we return to the States. I'm terribly proud of her.

Check and Balance

And then the cycle—weekly if not more often—when things seem to fall apart. We become overwhelmed by people's needs and problems and misunderstandings, by their taking offense and changing their position in matters of faith and the Spirit. Over time, we nevertheless somehow manage to address and repair and move beyond. Such difficulties are compounded by our failure to have more discretion and observe strict confidentiality in conducting the affairs of the kingdom.

Which raises that delicate question: When, though one ought to and is expected to, is one acting in a truly inspired manner and not in an arbitrary fashion? When is one truly just? In rendering a certain decision, I thought I was. In not foreseeing that others would prematurely disclose it, I was not. The subjective result was the same: we may have lost a valuable member and his family who had reason to think he would receive an important calling but did not.

Then there is the important consideration that even though such decisions may at times be arbitrary, their appointed source's right and need to make them should be honored. Otherwise, chaos may ensue. There is of course the ever-present possibility that innocent error, personal preference, or even unrighteous dominion might be exercised. How does the Church ingeniously help us to cope with the authority syndrome? In part, by making authorities of so many of us in turn. Additionally, we are less disposed toward unrighteous dominion by being released after a certain interval and by knowing that that will eventually happen.

Touché

A vivacious, young female member was recently impelled to see me about having her name removed so she could pursue another lifestyle with a clear conscience. I congratulated her on her candor, then surprised myself by proposing she prepare herself to go on a mission and have a real adventure. Similarly, one of our district presidents, Kondratev, approached the man who had been unwilling to sustain him at a recent conference and asked the man to serve with him as his secretary. The man readily consented.

Critical Choices

It has dawned on me that what we all face, all the time, is a choice between two paths—one higher, with steeper terrain, where you often strain to catch your breath or to reach a handhold, and another that lies well below it and tends if anything toward a gradual and easy descent. What we need at all times to bear in mind when serving one another is that we can either encourage each other to choose the higher, more difficult path or judgmentally write one another off for being the way we indeed often are. The Spirit lifts, we say—if, that is, we allow it to have its way.

Readiness

When repentance occurs, change is for all of us more a process than anything instantaneous, though there may be exceptions, such as those we see in certain converts. I suspect that their personal self-dissatisfaction had reached the point that, upon meeting the missionaries, they were already prepared to accept and quickly adopt what we have to offer them. Just as often we encounter those who seem to have been living and thinking all their lives in terms of our message. For these, the transition seems to involve little more than saying yes and following their inclination to engage in the Church's collective enterprise.

Full Surrender

In the work here and in ongoing relationships, those missionaries (and members) who *fully* give themselves up to their callings and who try to do their best are happy and fulfilled and properly rewarded. They want to do what they're asked because they sufficiently respect and trust their leaders and the cause they serve. Or at least they trust God, the ultimate source of it all. The Spirit has intervened in their lives, no less than in the lives of their investigators, to change and motivate how they think and act. In their gratitude and guilelessness, they manifest a "broken heart" and a "contrite

Courtesy Michael Hertig

Uniformed invasion. Missionaries on Palace Square sport the elders' standard summer dress: white shirt, tie, and no jacket. *From left:* Traver Maxwell, Matthew Palmer, David Wilcox, Stewart Peay, Christian Kaelin, and Donald Allison.

spirit" that make the Atonement accessible to them. They do not feel superior and are not self-satisfied, nor are they restless and in need of too many personal distractions.

They are obedient and supportive. They are helpful and willing to put themselves out for others. They aren't grasping, seeking more than their share of things at others' expense. They don't murmur and find fault. They don't unduly and hypersensitively suspect others' motives. They don't collude, and they are not duplicitous or manipulative. They don't scapegoat or project their frustrated, subconscious yearnings for recognition by criticizing others with particular callings. They are oblivious to the positions others hold or may yet hold. That is less important to them than magnifying their own callings, which for them are sufficiently important and challenging. They are humble and endear themselves to others. They love and are loved, despite the deficiencies of all involved.

On the other hand, those who are not so committed are simply not happy and in their frustration seek ways around what they were called here to do. Their goodwill and their magnanimity erode. They stay aloof and do not spontaneously or genuinely smile—except with those they consider allies and with whom they like to buddy and smirk, discussing what is wrong with others. They are worse than the most petty, gossipy old women. They have not yet learned to "put away childish things" (1 Cor. 13:11). What they do is serious and sinful, though they do not realize it and would doubtless be offended if told so. (It's one thing to keep failing and care about it but quite another to default and not care at all.) They see no particular connection between the personal license they take and their dissident opinions. They certainly do not seek to be guided in their mundane actions by the Lord's will. Their more conscientious companions are often devastated. I am readily reminded of Nephi's older brothers, of the unconverted Alma the Younger, and of the four sons of Mosiah.

There seem to be real consequences for those put under covenant whenever they do not consecrate themselves—when they do not exert all their "heart, might, mind and strength" (D&C 4:2). Missionaries understand this well enough with respect to those they interview for baptism and later encourage to enter the temple. But do all missionaries realize that the white handbook involves further covenants that apply just as much to them during this totally undisrupted and (perhaps for that reason) singularly trying, yet privileged, period in the Lord's service? Much as I fear for my own future, I fear even more for the futures of the few missionaries I have in mind.

High Goal

From Mary's journal:

> Earlier this week, I got to see new missionaries give the discussions to my parents. It was very educational since I'm trying to learn them as well. Some of the missionaries were so nervous I felt bad for them. Not only did they have to carry themselves well, project their voice, and maintain eye contact (a lot like acting), but they had to worry about correct pronunciation and grammar in front of a Russian professor. But my dad is a good coach, however intimidating he might be. I'm afraid I won't be satisfied now if my presentation of the first principle is anything less than perfect.

That They Might Have Joy

The missionaries need to feel better about themselves if they are doing all they can. The term "real intent" (Moro. 10:4) leaps out at us in the Book of Moroni. Though they have strong testimonies, many missionaries—and members generally—have yet to internalize what Christ's Atonement really means to them. They fail to see how it should buoy up their lives in times of disappointment or stress or testing. They have yet to understand that the Savior's grace should attend them with that "mighty change in [their] hearts," that they should then radiate joy with "his image in [their] countenances" (Alma 5:14). We will challenge the missionaries to consider the topic "My relationship with the Savior: how his Atonement helps sustain me as a joyful missionary."

Stephen Robinson's book *Believing Christ* (Deseret Book, 1992) is a real eye-opener in this regard. We need to better understand the relationship between the concepts of perfection, atonement, desire, repentance, and so forth. One of our new branch presidents touchingly described his experience this way: "We were taught only to hate our enemies. The Church is a school of love."

Getting out the kinks. As they gather for a Fourth of July celebration, these joyful missionaries learn how to play hard as well as work hard. *Left to right, on the ground:* Darren Chamberlain, Christopher Eastland, Matthew Fisher, Michael Morrison, and two unidentified elders. *Standing,* John Bradshaw, Christopher Preston, Grant Beckwith, and one more unidentified elder.

Courtesy John Valentine

I was similarly affected upon reading an excerpt from the dying New York critic Alfred Kazin's memoirs, entitled "Jews," in *The New Yorker* (March 7, 1994, 62–73). I've shared with the missionaries his thoughtful observation that the lot of humankind is universal loneliness—reminding them that in *this* world metropolis of cultural wonders and tragic contrasts, not unlike New York City, the missionaries have assisted people to transcend such loneliness and to learn it is not inevitable.

Northern Exposure

After meeting the Morgans at the airport—the missionary couple who will introduce seminaries and institutes in our mission—we thought to bring them to a local hotel restaurant for a meal in the company of President and Sister Efimov. For some reason, I was the only one facing the cleared floor space in the room's center. All went well, the food tasty enough. Then suddenly everyone noticed the startled look on my face. A bevy of tall young ladies had suddenly assembled behind our guests—the evening's entertainment. Their upper bodies were skimpily swathed in what looked like long, diaphanous feathers, but it was what seemed missing elsewhere that had so stunned me. When the others in our party saw the unseemly spectacle, we rose in unison from our table and, without touching the dessert, made our way to the exit along the room's periphery. Our predicament was so ludicrous that first one of us, then all the others broke into fairly audible giggles before we could beat a quick retreat. Thus were the Morgans initiated to the new Russia.

Living Lessons: Autumn 1994

Many Hands

I still often despair when I anticipate the outcome of some necessary confrontation or the resolution of some circumstance involving the members. Such despair is a kind of sin and usually proves unfounded. The solution so often comes in the form of others with whom I counsel, leaders who are ready and willing and knowledgeable and wise. With or through them, I can successfully address the issue I'm facing.

Illusions

Witnessing the following events has led me to an important realization:

- blessings to missionaries overwhelmed by fear and doubt after unexpectedly witnessing a sudden death
- the default of investigators who tell themselves they cannot give up smoking or alcohol or that they have "fallen out of love" with the spouse with whom they must still share the same roof
- occasional serious discord between missionaries who, in their scapegoating, attribute to one another the most malicious motives, the most heinous character.

My realization: the assumptions underlying these problems all fall short of our true nature and potential, of reality in the ideal, eternal sense. By buying into illusions that are, by their very nature, empty, cold, and void of light, whose ultimate author is "the father of all lies" (2 Ne. 2:18), we instead underestimate what we or others can actually do or be. Truly, as Paul suggests, we deal with "principalities and powers" (Col. 2:15), whose presence or absence is more apparent in Russia, where neutrality and ambiguity are still too much of a luxury.

Mikhail Lermontov's poem of 1831 seems especially appropriate.

We drink from the cup of existence
With closed eyes,

Wetting its gold rim
With our tears;
When at our death
The veil falls from our eyes

And everything that deluded us
Disappears with that veil,
Then we see that
The gold beaker was empty,
That its beverage was a dream,
And that it is not ours!

Leveler

Another great blessing that all missionaries need to recognize is that a mission simply makes them more aware of their personal inadequacies. Such recognition is an important first step in doing something about those imperfections. Equally important, when more acutely aware of their weaknesses, missionaries need to maintain a fundamental love and respect for themselves. This is easier to do when we understand that perfection is a process rather than some definitive achievement, here and perhaps in the next world too.

C'est la vie

Returning early to their apartment recently, a pair of missionaries encountered a young couple who had already ransacked their belongings and stuffed the stolen clothing into the elders' empty suitcases. Dropping their booty, then nonchalantly walking past the elders and out of the apartment, the man called back, "*Byvaet*" ("Such is life").

Casualties

To date, I've had to send four missionaries home on medical leave and had one more reassigned stateside who could not adequately learn the language. At the moment, three others are abroad—in Hamburg and Helsinki—receiving medical treatment. Another elder would like to leave before the end of his mission for further medical assistance, if that were possible. The diagnoses of those we have sent home appear to vindicate our having done so. The other diagnoses (a cyst that would not heal brought on by an infected hair follicle; a peptic ulcer and hiatal hernia, likely aggravated by hyperactive syndrome; and a shattered finger caused by "slam dunking" on p-day) all seemed to require more reliable Western medical attention.

Trivial disruptions impede what we were sent here to do.

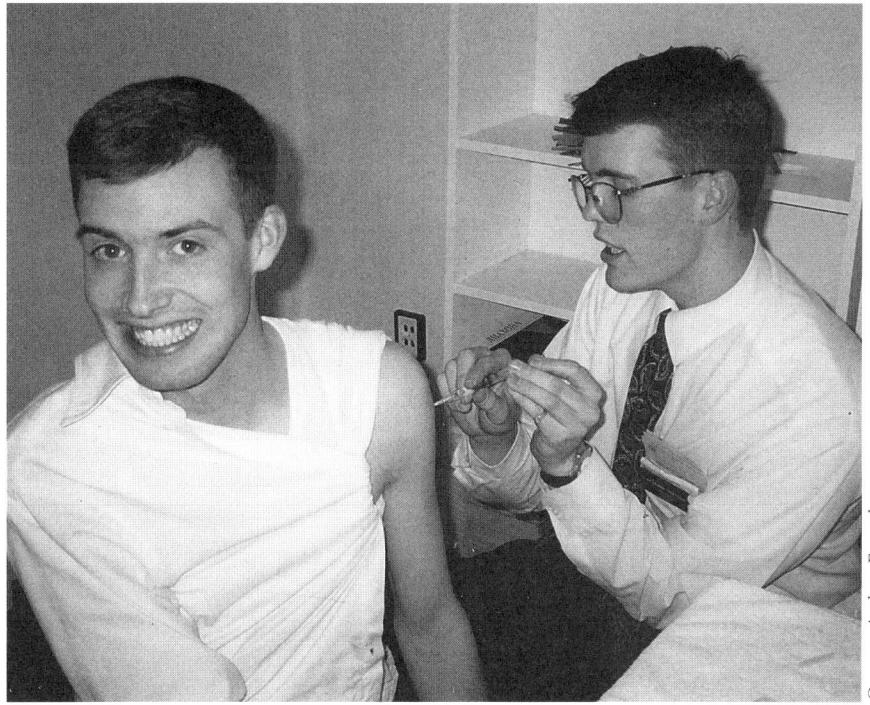

Courtesy Andrew Eversole

Time for shots. Elder Andrew Eversole plays doctor to Elder John Valentine. Missionaries receive gamma globulin twice a year to maintain their resistance to infections. One custodian accused them of using drugs.

For the Long Term

The most inactive tend to be members of longer standing. It's almost as if they've passed their two-year membership course and gotten out of it what they were meant to—their diploma, as it were—and can now return to their former lifestyle. An important challenge is that we convert new investigators more fully and that they take on membership with open eyes: they need to understand that they are making eternal covenants with the Lord and with no one else and to take those covenants that seriously. Because too many were lapsing in regard to the Word of Wisdom, we now authorize people to be baptized only after they have abstained from smoking or drinking for at least a month. We also require them to attend church at least three times, hopefully all three meetings for three Sundays in a row. I also ask the missionaries to inform converts that, as they join the Church, they must be willing to accept callings, including that of home or visiting teacher.

Undue Burden

In interviews, I frequently discover that abuse by or the negligence of an alcoholic husband or father has led to great suffering and deprivation. I had to interview one investigator because she feared she had "murdered" her youngest child four years ago. She explained that in a bout of depression over her husband's drinking she had taken an overdose of sleeping pills and while she slept her unattended child had fallen to his death from an upper-story window. Even the neighbors blamed her. I tried to reassure her that she was the victim of circumstances (primarily of her husband's drinking) and had in no way intended those consequences.

Courtesy Michael Hertig

Alcoholic's apartment. Drugs, alcohol, and poverty have eroded the Russian family.

Apron Strings

The Russians' possessive-mother syndrome is clearly manifest in a number of families we have come to know. In its excess, this tendency is very unhealthy. It creates suffocating codependencies on the part of married children and exacerbates conflicts with their spouses. This syndrome is particularly noticeable when, as often happens, all are forced to live under the same roof. In so many cases, through death, drinking, abandonment, or outright divorce, husbands are a thing of the past. And my sense is that, by overindulging and never emancipating their sons, who, in the absence of other men, are at every age the center of these women's lives, such mothers encourage those same sons to expect that the women they marry will do everything for them. At least Russian women care. If anything, they care too much, while the men don't care nearly enough. There is a terrible imbalance here, and the concept of partnership in marriage is something we badly need to teach our members.

Brother's Keepers

From Elder Justin Stratton's journal:

With the Howards [American members; the father is a chiropractor with paramedical experience], we went to see my old investigator Aleksey play in a soccer tournament. We showed up right at the end of the last game and missed his. That was unfortunate, but it was still good we came. We waited for Aleksey to change, and then we all returned together.

While we were on the metro, the young man sitting near us went into what we thought was a seizure but ended up being a heart attack. Since Brother Howard is a doctor, we tried to help out. First we got the young man off the metro car and called an ambulance, and then Brother Howard started doing CPR. A Russian came over and did the breathing. For the first ten minutes, they kept the guy going. He was only about 25 years old. A lady who worked in the metro gave the guy two shots, one of adrenaline and one of something else.

We carried on for about thirty minutes before the ambulance showed up. Brother Howard said the guy needed EKG (electric shock), but when the EMT's got there and we jumped out of the way, they just stood around and watched. They didn't take over the CPR or anything. This annoyed us so bad that we decided to walk off. A girl stopped us and asked what needed to be done. We said the guy needed DFIB. They didn't have the needed instruments and just gave us a dumb look. They didn't even check the pulse. They just gave up on him.

As we walked away in frustration, it really hit me how little they value life in this country. Even if the EMTs couldn't do anything, if they'd hurried to the guy instead of walking and had tried to do something, it wouldn't have been so bad. But they were just earning their money for the day, as revealed by the way they were dressed and carried themselves. The guy was with two friends, and one ran after us and gave Brother Howard two icons. Brother Howard didn't want them, but the man insisted and said his friend would have wanted him to take them.

As we got back on the metro, we were all fairly shaken. Brother Howard was sad for the people and their whole situation, and Aleksey seemed troubled too. First, he was sad for his country, and second, I think it made him think a little more about death. I hope it will help him investigate the Church more.

Well-Wishers

A kind, professorial couple, the Alimovs, have befriended Merriam and me, perhaps in part to have someone on whom to practice their already accomplished English. Mrs. Alimov is a diplomat's daughter who attended high school in New York. She seems more open to the Church than her husband. He has traveled to Antarctica and teaches world history as a general education offering at the Meteorological Institute. She has taught English in secondary schools. He suffers from clinical depression. Their grown son and daughter seem, in a contemporary fashion, quite distant from the parents. As Mrs. Alimov put it to me, she and her husband, as stalwart Party members, earlier had something to live for—a purpose—but no more. Still, I fear that—typical of their class—they would find it too scandalous to their intellectual friends and possibly too much effort to investigate the Church in any serious fashion.

Bad Call

I often think of the accusation that we are all robots, all sheep. Then I look at what rugged individuals our outstanding members have to be in this environment, how self-denying and committed and discerning our leaders have to be. At every step, each must exercise initiative along with constant inspiration. How mature all must be to work together in team fashion (and by contrast how egotistical and self-centered those are who cannot or will not). Then I have to smile at how *dead wrong* many of the Church's critics are, both within and outside the fold. Of course, common agreement on and full acceptance of certain fundamental principles is presupposed. But what's so wrong with that if they're also true principles—and the Lord's? That's reason enough to defer to those who have stewardship over the institution that so assiduously encourages us to live the gospel, both individually and together.

Building morale among members. District President Vyacheslav Kondratev (*standing front left*) and several participants gather at a mission youth conference. Such events build lasting friendships that help members withstand the adversity and pressure of the secular world.

This observation leads me to a keener sense of why intellectuals rarely join the Church: in their versatile, resilient minds they can, under any circumstances, too readily distract themselves. Others, less verbally or conceptually disposed, are more vividly aware of their limitations—for which life's cruder, more obvious forms of escape clearly do not compensate. The life of the mind and the aesthetic sense are, moreover, such powerful and comprehensive surrogates, such subtle spiritual imitations (and often as not religion's legitimate enhancements) that intellectuals can remain too easily distracted, too comfortable, and too self-satisfied.

Celestial Vision

Unexpectedly, on a recent Sunday evening, a steady stream of fairly recent members came to the office for last-Sunday-of-the-month interviews. Included in the group were a score of young men who had been encouraged by their local leaders to prepare for the higher priesthood. Each young man had radically and unhesitatingly, even gratefully, altered his life for the privilege of serving God and blessing others' lives. In these whole-souled Russians, I was witnessing the dynamic consecration of lives. I could envision a number of the branches doubling almost overnight in their leadership strength and potential.

Sacred Singularity

A thought occurred to me recently as, one by one, missionaries were bearing their testimonies. Their various weaknesses and points of vulnerability cover a broad spectrum indeed and are in some cases recognizable only after a long and fairly intimate acquaintance with each missionary. Nevertheless, each missionary is particularly appealing for being so distinctively him- or herself. One would not want any of them to be other than they in fact distinctly are—nor could they be.

Labyrinth

After two more elders were robbed during the same period, a call came to us late in the night from police investigators who insisted we provide a native translator, since the elders could not read the investigators' handwritten report before cosigning. I told the investigators we would trust them. That would not do. I asked them to read the report aloud to the elders.

That would not do either because the elders could not be sure the investigators were reading back to them what they had written.

I told the police we could not produce a translator for them at 2:00 A.M. But the next day would be the inspectors' day off. And the day after that would be our driver-interpreter's day off. And so it went—this overly cautious concern for protecting their skirts. Perhaps it is symptomatic of a long-conditioned unwillingness to take initiative beyond already clearly defined parameters—to the ultimate disadvantage of those they were meant to serve.

The social evils here that so confine and oppress individual lives are clearly traceable to all that transpired after 1917, but derive as much from the injustices that also prevailed here for many centuries. Is the spirit and worldview of Salt Lake City very different from what it was a hundred years ago—a strong core of stability and monolithic devotion, contested by Gentiles and the disenchanted? Similarly, St. Petersburg.

Courtesy Mary Rogers

Standing drunk. Alcoholism and midday inebriation are common social problems throughout Russia.

So much that still occurs here seems a flashback to the life Dostoevsky wrote about. Like no other Russian author, he focused on the "insulted and injured." Reading him, one might easily wonder if it isn't all an exaggeration, the projection of his own hysteria—or at best a penetrating theological abstraction, a valuable though figurative reading of everyone's soul (which it most certainly is). But it also reflects to us the country's daily reality nearly 130 years after the publication of *Crime and Punishment*—the alcoholism, the rampant crime, the neglect of the young. Not to mention the cramped living space that often requires young couples to cohabit with older parents and in-laws—a major cause of marital discontent and divorce.

Complacent

From Mary's journal:

> When I returned to the States, I was on a high whenever I thought of the things I couldn't enjoy while I was in Russia. For instance, the day I got home, I went to the apartment kitchen to get a drink of cold, clean water straight out of the tap. As I finished it, I turned to my roommates and said, "Look! I can drink it straight from the tap, and I don't have to worry about getting giaradia! I can even brush my teeth with tap water!" But my roommates didn't share my enthusiasm. They just looked at me like I was crazy.

Foreboding Event

The Russian military's recent invasion of Chechnya has demoralized almost everyone I talk to. It further intensifies the pressure on men of draft age, keeping more of our otherwise eligible young priesthood bearers from serving missions.

Humbling

When I consider that the Savior's entire earthly mission was also for only three years, and ours is now nearly half over, I blanch to realize how very little we have accomplished in his name.

Toughing It Out: Winter 1995

Samaritans?

It was a dark, chill, winter night with deep snow. Our spirits were warmed, however, by the baptisms we'd just attended at a nicely decorated sauna on the outskirts of town. There were eight or nine baptisms that evening, with many missionaries and members in attendance. A group of young sisters even serenaded us with Russian folk songs as we walked out to the mission van—and it seemed so right: hymns for the service, native refrains afterward, reminding us of the rich culture of those who have come into the Church. An inspiring amalgam! As we drove away, those soulful Russian melodies echoed in our heads, warming us further, together with our thoughts about those who, arrayed in white, had just entered the Lord's kingdom. It was a truly beatific moment, reinforced by the newly fallen snow's pure whiteness. Life was suddenly very, very good.

We had not passed through too many intersections, however, before we suddenly noticed the figure of a woman lying prostrate near the curb. On this occasion, we did not hesitate to stop the van and render assistance. Were she to lie there much longer, she would surely perish from exposure. But she did not lift easily. Nor could she stand without our assistance. She was probably in her late forties, and she was completely drunk. Luckily, my two missionary assistants were with us and helped guide her to the van, where we settled her between Merriam and me.

As we drove farther, we were anxious to know where she lived or at least where we could safely deliver her. We never got a satisfactory reply, though she conversed volubly, venting her muddy thoughts and her hysterical grief for a soldier son who had recently died in Chechnya. For this she blamed Yeltsin. Then, detecting that we were not Russians, she began to flail her arms, implicating us too. Merriam had tried to express our condolences, which only fueled the woman's ire. "I will kill you!" she threatened. Then, with yet another wild toss of the arm, she smacked me in the jaw.

I want to think that frustration rather than mere annoyance prompted me to order our driver to stop the van. There was, after all, no way to know our guest's address or where to bring her, and she was now at least warmed by the van's heater and, so long as she kept moving, well insulated in her long fur coat. So we escorted her to an adjacent sidewalk, hoping she'd remain upright and others in the neighborhood would, if need be, come to her aid. Perhaps they would know how to handle her better. Once more, our feeble attempt to be Samaritans had left us with the deepest sense of failure, while our euphoric memory of the baptisms and the resonant folk songs had in the meantime considerably dimmed.

Quality Control

Right now I have two large concerns: (1) making sure Sunday School and priesthood teachers present engaging lessons rather than giving dull, soporific monologues or reading every line from *Gospel Essentials,* a practice which is still common. How can we expect a regular three-hour-long attendance from any investigator—let alone any but the most devoted members—under such circumstances? And (2) having all the branch leaders aware of and concerned about both individual members (ministry) and organizational matters (administration).

Criterion

After every sacrament meeting talk and every Sunday School lesson, we should know each other a little better—so that we can care more about each other. The purpose of our recurring meetings must be to that end as well as to "pump us up," as some missionaries put it. We worship together not for ourselves alone but for a number of particular others.

Formulas

It is most likely the nature of almost all men once they become contemplative to make up lists or formulas of dos and don'ts to cover all possible contingencies. I'm no different. I've thought up many such and expounded them to the members and missionaries. The most powerful mathematical equations, we are told, are both the simplest and most comprehensive. At this point, I've reduced my slogans for the missionaries to the following:

- Engage the Spirit.
- Personally testify.
- Utilize the members.
- Love the people you meet.

I've also told the missionaries that they can enjoy this work, however much they are rejected, if they will do only two things: (1) be curious about and interested in the people they meet—each one a unique and complex being—and (2) as they try to curl their tongues around Russian words and make themselves understood, become fascinated by the language's exotic sounds and weird idioms.

To Catch a Thief

From Elder Christopher Preston:

> This last week, we had a really crazy experience. My companion's boots were stolen, and we had to chase down the thief. We were in the mission office when a man who had been visited by the missionaries came by to get more information about the Church. He seemed to spend a lot of time near the shelves where we all put our boots. Suddenly we noticed that he was gone.
>
> Elder Chad Smith had an uneasy feeling that the man might have taken his new boots. We counted all the boots, and everything seemed in order. Elder Smith noticed that his boots had been moved

Courtesy Chris James

Missionaries at orphanage hospital. Full-time missionaries Elders Jaroslav Rzezanka and Christopher James spent time working with sick children. Missionaries serve the communities where they work. Lending a hand to the elderly and sick are popular service projects.

and then realized that they weren't even his boots. The man had traded a pair of old worn-out boots for Elder Smith's new ones.

Instantly, we decided to run out to the street, hoping we could locate the thief. At first we thought he had gotten away, but then we saw someone running across the next canal bridge. It was our man! Without coats and still wearing slippers, the two of us tore down the snow swept street. Ties flapping in the wind, feet sliding all over the ice, we crossed the bridge and began to gain on him.

Elder Smith got to him first and asked him what he had in his bag. At first the man denied he had even been at the office. Finally, he confessed and opened his bag. There were Elder Smith's boots along with a copy of the *Liahona* and a few other Church publications. The man was wearing a second, decent pair of boots he'd brought with him to the office.

It must have been a sight to see two young men in white shirts, the Lord's emissaries, racing down the snowy street after such a trivial thing as a pair of boots. I almost wish we hadn't gone after them. It felt wrong. How bad off do you have to be to steal a pair of boots? Or to reclaim them?

More Hassle?

Yesterday's elections to the duma would appear, like the political crisis last October, to spell doom for the Church here. At least that's the view of our senior district president. Our Russian lawyer feels that it's just another blip on the radar screen. Again, Russia faces a quagmire of uncertainty about her future. At least it keeps things interesting during the long, dreary winter, which, perhaps understandably, too many try to endure with alcohol.

Russian Colonel Kanes

Notably, two more local nonmembers have befriended us. One is Volodya Korolyov, a science professor who voluntarily heads up a support group for the over ten thousand inmates at St. Petersburg's notorious holding prison, *Kresty* (The Cross). The Church has assisted him with clothing, blankets, and basic medical supplies. In gratitude he wanted to present us with a cat of a rare Russian breed. It was hard to decline this hospitable gesture, but we felt it inappropriate to keep animals in a Church facility.

The other is Aleksandr Veyrauch. A Russian ascetic and pure idealist, Aleksandr purposely champions our presence in Russia as a protest against the institutional monopolization of religious thought. This despite the fact that the Spaulding theory—which he's read about and which I tell him is a dated objection—prevents his believing that the Book of Mormon and Joseph Smith are what we claim. He's arranged for me to deliver at least three papers on LDS theology at scholarly gatherings. The attendance is generally slight, the response tepid (reminiscent of the professional conferences I'm used to in my own discipline). This indifference, I believe, is not because those present are put off by Mormonism. Rather, like so many intellectuals, each is totally wrapped up in his own investigations and is primarily there to be heard rather than to listen to others.

Reason Together

I've been told the word is out that I can be "sweet-talked" into accommodating the missionaries' wishes much of the time regarding transfers, changes of companionship, and so forth. And that is true, if the "sweet talk" persuades me. What I find distressing is that such accommodation is perceived as uninspired, as if revelation must always come as one-way communication and bolts of "Zap"—"Do this or else!" Can't we extend sufficient respect and trust to consider others' preferences and aspirations in rendering decisions in their behalf? Can't we even learn from and be advised by those for whom we have stewardship?

I think we have lost sight of certain scriptural injunctions that suggest we need to "reason together . . . even as a man reasoneth one with another face to face" (D&C 50:10–11). And we ignore at our peril Joseph Smith's own sentiments:

> When persons manifest the least kindness and love to me, O what power it has over my mind, while the opposite course has a tendency to harrow up all the harsh feelings and depress the human mind.
>
> If you do not accuse each other, God will not accuse you. . . . If you will throw a cloak of charity over my sins, I will over yours—for charity covereth a multitude of sins. (*Teachings of the Prophet Joseph Smith*, Deseret Book, 1972, 240, 193)

Here again, the Prophet's teachings show a practical application of the two greatest commandments.

He Understands

How would you react if you discovered you'd buried an endowed sister still wearing her black pumps or been served the sacrament by Primary kids still too young to be deacons? Such things doubtless happen in every mission field—a cause for initial dismay and strong impetus to learn from those mistakes. Still, I tell myself, such things are somehow tolerable to the Lord, who, if no one else, will understand.

Ouch!

Sister M weighs on my mind. She is a professor's widow, recently robbed by another seemingly upstanding member, wonderfully hospitable to our son Will, her sickly son being his same age. Why did I so ineptly handle her negative "vote" in a sacrament meeting when we asked the members to sustain a new branch president? "I don't object to the new man," she said. "I just feel bad for the one you released." Which prompted me to lecture her—in that very public setting—about what it means to sustain. If she was not humiliated, I certainly felt officious. I spoke to her afterward, as casually and kindly as possible. Still learning!

Powers and Principalities

From Elder Lyall Swim:

> If I didn't know the devil was against us, I do now. We've been working hard, but Satan is using those great tools discouragement and guilt. As I lay in bed last night, I was overcome with darkness and despair. I didn't want to pray. I just wanted to go home. But like the Prophet Joseph, as I was about to give up, I made one last effort and commanded the darkness to leave. Then peace came. I didn't have a vision, but I learned what the Lord means in Ether 12:27: "Then will I make weak things become strong." I felt that strength and knew the Lord had confidence in me. I could not and would not let him down.

Memorable Moment

From Elder Ryan Dent:

> Very recently I met a young man, named Vova, who was soon to be baptized. My companion, Elder Wayne Guymon, was giving him the interview for baptism. The next day the baptism was held at a *banya*. When the time came to confirm him, the missionary performing the ordinance leaned over Vova's shoulder to ask who he would like to stand in the circle. One by one, the missionaries Vova named came

forward. Then Vova looked in my general direction and motioned for still one more to join them. I looked around me, but by his expression, Vova assured me I was the one he wanted to be in the circle. I'll never forget the gesture of a twelve-year-old boy to a missionary, inviting him to assist him to receive the Holy Ghost. It would touch the heart of that missionary forever.

Inequalities

During a recent missionwide preparation-day basketball playoff, I was struck that the two teams that emerged in the finals were almost to the man made up of our present or previous Zone Leaders and Assistants to the President. Their superior agility seems, along with the discipline they've managed to demonstrate in athletics, to have carried over to what makes them so outstanding here. Were they always that way—infants with remarkable eye-hand coordination?

What of those who stood on the sideline in suits, looking for all the world like their coaches, but not playing because they lacked the same skill or disposition? (I'd have been one of those in my young missionary days.) Does their musical or other training count for as much? And what of those relatively few who have no particular skill training whatsoever and were—as their fitful mastery of the language and discussions attests—always mediocre students? Whose fault is that? Dare any of us really say?

Perhaps the answer lies in the indisputable fact of life that we are in many respects not equal and that there is not, nor can there be, any earthly justice. This circumstance in turn creates the need, and opportunity, for people to be there for one another: "'Who did sin, this man or his parents, that he was born blind?' 'Neither hath this man sinned, nor his parents: but that the works of God should be made manifest in him'" (John 9:2–3).

Universal Language

This week we look forward to the arrival of Darrell and Eva Stubbs, our latest missionary couple, both professional musicians, for the inspiring enhancement they will bring to our worship. (Perhaps they'll help us rival those Orthodox priests who intone their liturgy with such an impressive, booming bass or baritone. The arts have their place in worship and p.r.— "Fight fire with fire!")

Which reminds me of that extraordinary and otherwise superfluous moment in Chekhov's *Seagull* where a minor character describes the occasion during his younger years when a famous choir came to their village. The choir's renowned soloist, Silvio, had the deepest bass voice in the land. At the end of one particular rendition, after Silvio had outdone himself by descending to his very deepest, prolonged note, the astounded audience then heard from some nameless peasant in the audience a lengthy, heartfelt "Bravo, Silvio"—delivered still an octave lower.

[The Stubbs "delivered" for us with wonderful woodwind concerts and programs by the mission choir. As, in their fashion, did our faithful office couples—Dee and Pat Hubbard, Ray and Patricia Banks, Bill and Jessie Martell—and our marvelous seminary-institute coordinators—first Don

Courtesy Andrew Eversole

Missionary couple. Elder Darrell and Sister Eva Stubbs orchestrated woodwind concerts and also instructed the mission choir.

and Shirley Morgan, then Otis and Donna Romriel, and finally Gail and Alta Halvorsen. These were all preceded by a pioneering proselyting couple, long-time residents of Alaska, Von and Suzanne Mitten.]

Grim

I learned with dismay that a recent convert, Vladislav, just died from a bad heart; he was only in his forties. Unmarried, apparently without family, he was a wistful, dwarflike poet, almost childlike in his response to the gospel and his new friends. He'd told us about the heart problem before his baptism. He'd even feared what entering the cold water might do to him. Rather inauspiciously, I'd jestingly promised to attend his funeral if the ordinance in fact killed him. Each Sunday thereafter he read to us in the sacrament service a newly written poem celebrating his joy in the gospel.

I decided the Church must pay for his burial and requested that some of his poems be read at the service. For just such occasions, I had bought myself a $20 black suit at Savers. Somehow though, a black suit didn't quite fit the cherubic, life-affirming Vladislav, whose brief, enthusiastic coming among us had proved so inspirational.

The funeral itself—on a cold, winter day at Petersburg's crematorium—was in its impersonality and crude disposal of the corpse shocking indeed. The open and doubtless recycled casket that displayed him was no more than thin plywood with a garish vermilion crepe-paper border. At the brief ceremony's conclusion, the stern officiator—as at State weddings, invariably a woman—pressed some button or pulled a lever that bumpily whisked Vladislav and his coffin to the flames that awaited him in the nether world a floor below.

Involuntarily, we tried to catch our collective breath as one does in some elevators or during a roller coaster's sudden descent. There he was; then in the very next moment, with no warning, not even a musical decrescendo, *he wasn't*. Nor as we left the mausoleum did we dare imagine what the chunks of light-hued ash might be that, for better traction, workers had tossed onto the steep icy path we trod upon. But Vladislav would have understood. He would have just laughed, delighted for our company despite the grim circumstances.

Aging

I've just returned from a conference in Moscow with the Area Presidency and other mission presidents. The thirty-six hour round trip involved, besides our meetings, travel through heavy traffic to and from the two airports, waiting in long lines at every step, and dealing with a multitude of unfamiliar logistics and surroundings. For the first time in my life, I felt that I am no longer young. In fact, I suddenly felt very, very old. Yet almost every day the Seventies put themselves through as demanding a routine, not to mention the Quorum of the Twelve.

Shocker

The most violent incident involving our missionaries—hopefully an isolated event—has been the taking of five of them and a district president hostage. A gang of martial arts hoodlums who had earlier taunted some of them on the street accosted them during a sacrament service. The elders were first kicked and struck on the head, then forced to lie face down on the floor, execution style. The hoodlums, approximately twelve in number, confiscated their documents and personal property. All the while, one of the gang, a man in his forties, took careful inventory in an all too professional manner. Luckily, a member who arrived late managed to summon the police before more took place. (The intruders were carrying whips and who knows what else in canvas bags.)

The police allowed all but three of the gang to get away. The missionaries thereupon underwent longer detention and interrogation than the aggressors. The first investigating officer seemed utterly indifferent, if not in fact partial to the thugs. The thugs meanwhile arranged to have a sensational TV station film them and the elders at the police station. Still later, they gave libelous interviews to two local papers that refused to print our own refutation of their charges against the Church.

The five elders offered no resistance during the incident. They testify that they remained perfectly calm and had never felt the Spirit more strongly than on that occasion. Two of the missionaries' contacts who had attended the meeting that Sunday were baptized the next week. Finally, a new investigating officer came along, bent on fully bringing the offenders to justice.

What's the Secret?

Just last night, we heard Shostakovich's Seventh Symphony, composed to commemorate the million victims of the Nazi blockade who perished in this very city. Earlier we'd caught his eleventh, which recalls the Bloody Sunday massacre of 1905 that took place just a stone's throw away on Winter Palace Square. An audience of thousands—strangers to each other—leaned forward in the balconies or sat otherwise riveted, completely enthralled. Why can't we reach these people, so susceptible to the arts, with the equally sublime and universally significant message of the restored gospel? Where do we fail to touch their very touchable hearts?

Steadying the Ark: Spring 1995

Solicitations

The Gypsy children are out vying for the attention of Western tourists with their touchy-feely contacting approach, intent of course on robbing their victims blind. Sometimes one of them pokes you with a needle while others go for your pockets during the momentary distraction.

Then there are the nice-looking young men and women of missionary age who congregate early each morning in front of our office. They wear Western-made, white windbreakers whose logos advertise Rothman's "quality" cigarettes. (The ads fail to mention the tobacco itself is from Bulgaria and not the prestigious West.) Stinking up our hallway as they light their own, they then go eagerly forth with free packs to hook Petersburg's young—their particular *Agitation for Happiness*.

Clearly, our own agitation for happiness has more worthy and longlasting ends. Though we may distress some people as much as do the Gypsies, our message fills the breast with a most rare and precious (nicotine-free) *pneuma*.

Good Seed

The missionaries are discouraged right now. We were supposed to do better come spring, but in the last month, conversions have fallen off markedly. I must try to persuade the missionaries that there are still many out there like the several remarkable members they've already brought into the fold. Meanwhile, their own loving, serene, life-affirming presence does much to cheer and gladden and afford hope to even those who may reject their message. It is a good seed if the sowers themselves do not despair too much.

An Eye Single

I was challenged by a senior missionary (Elder A) about what he anticipated would be the pending call of another (Elder B) as my new assistant. Elder B, who has special gifts and a strong personality, may have alienated some who are less intense. I lost my cool and chastised Elder A for so

Messengers of hope. Sisters Donna Fluckiger (Simonson) and Jenna Hughes (Tew) radiate the Spirit. They are standing in front of the Moika River canal across from St. Isaac's Cathedral.

asserting his dislike and prejudice but held off calling Elder B for fear others might resent him. When I later did so, I charged him to be a peacemaker. In the aftermath, there seemed to be no difficulty. Moreover, after a relatively brief term as my assistant, Elder B himself asked me to "plow him back" into the force to serve once more as companion to an elder who was at that point deeply discouraged. The results were miraculous.

All Too Human

Prior to returning home, a senior elder asked others to mail him a package that apparently he couldn't fit in his luggage. As has been his custom, their district president, who frequently travels abroad, offered to mail the package while out of the country. This time he was intercepted at the border and required to open the package. It proved to contain two Russian passports, one with the now departed American elder's picture superimposed and laminated in place of that of the original Russian owner. "Who gave it to you?" they asked the innocent district president. Desperately, he recalled three missionaries' names, one of whom had not been involved. Within less than twenty-four hours, all three found themselves on U.S. soil and reassigned to stateside missions.

The elder who had altered the passports did so, I'm convinced, just to have a few special souvenirs. He has since suffered deep remorse and has implored the forgiveness of all affected. Now the test is ours—to see if each of us, including the three now stateside, will be sufficiently forgiving.

Adversity Humbles

What are they doing "right" in Kiev to enjoy every month twice as many baptisms as we do? And they have only thirty or so full-time proselytizing missionaries. [The Ukrainian powers-that-be severely restricted the issuing of visas to LDS missionaries during the period of our mission.] The Ukraine is far worse off economically. Does desperation help?

Need for Space

Certainly when there is any disharmony whatsoever, we lack that total unity without which we cannot have the Spirit or function as we ought.

The whole team effort is compromised. In this light, my latest diatribe about valiant and not-so-valiant missionaries has given me further pause. There are so many varied perspectives—as many as there seem to be people—generally quite sincerely held. Perhaps sincerity and honesty are also separate categories, but we all need space in which to work out our salvation. Even a missionary's agency and right to choose his actions need to be respected. I become irate only when those actions adversely impinge on the choices of others, such as junior companions. And that's another complicating factor: a missionary can't be a law unto himself because, basically, he never acts independently. And who does, really?

Replay

In an ultrachauvinistic manner, the occasional priesthood holder will still literally interpret Paul's counsel to the women as "Be silent. Submit yourself to your Lord (man-in-charge) and so address him." On the other hand, we have a high proportion of investigators and even some leaders whose wives harass and discourage them from being involved in the Church. In too many instances, women leaders contend with or try to dictate terms to their priesthood counterparts. It's like a replay of their own failed relations in marriage, projected onto people in the Church. Or a reversion to the way they responded as adolescents to their parents.

Grave Misconceptions

Problems arise when the head and the emotions are not sufficiently in tandem or properly informed and directed by transcendent powers. I've observed here that, in their mode of worship, many faiths tend either to a one-sided rationality—evangelical proof texting, humanistic aloofness, higher criticism—or its exact opposite—a nonrational, even nondiscursive mysticism, with the mind deliberately blunted or turned off. The latter tendency includes trance-induced worship, often involving a steady repetitious drumbeat, the counting of prayer beads, the repetition of the names of Deity or saints, or set prayers. This tendency is not unlike the altered state of mind induced by drugs or hard rock music.

By contrast, the scriptures of the restored Church clearly stress that both mind and heart must work together—implicitly decrying the false dichotomy that would separate feeling and reason. In the West, that di-chotomy is in part attributable to Plato's influence on Augustine and to Augustine's on everyone else, a stronger influence than many realize.

Traditional Christianity fails to understand two fundamental things: First, the true nature of scripture. For instance, fundamentalist Protestants make of the Bible a talisman and confine the living God to a book. Second, the intent of the essential Christian ordinances, baptism and communion. Despite the clear explanations in the New Testament, many denominations fail to understand that the very purpose of these ordinances is disavowed and rendered inefficacious when not intrinsically coupled with freely, knowledgeably, and worthily undertaken covenants. Such covenants in turn completely nullify infant baptism or automatic adherence to a state religion. These fundamental issues are not well understood because of the world's longstanding failure to adhere to a prophetic tradition.

Whose Church?

Increasingly, I sense why in the Church we need to have authorities and submit ourselves to their counsel. The dangers of unrighteous dominion are largely offset by those of unrighteous petitioning and advantage taking. A man we'd thought to call as a new branch president meanwhile resorted again to drink, physically abused the grown daughter he'd baptized just the week before, and so frightened his aged mother that she suffered a stroke. He then chopped off his finger in the presence of other members, and after consuming methyl alcohol, ended up almost expiring. After so losing con-trol, this same brother insisted that the Church would fall apart if he were not soon elevated to an important position.

As Elder Dennis B. Neuenschwander has pointed out, there is a ten-dency on the part of some to believe that the Church belongs to them rather than the opposite. I suspect this attitude is compounded by the fact that such individuals, though often capable enough, have up till now never been given a chance to take initiative, lead others, or prove themselves in any way. A few others, who like this man are clearly unstable, also seem to unhealthily enmesh themselves with those who have paid them more attention than they have ever received. Such codependers often seem to lack much sense of propriety and order.

Oops!

From Mary's journal:

> A couple of weeks ago, I was attending a sacrament meeting where one of the senior missionaries spoke about pride and judging others. Since he doesn't speak Russian, he had a translator assist him so the members would understand. The English-speaking members would hear and understand first, then after the translation, so would the Russians. At one point, the elder said, "Now when you find yourself judging someone, a red flag should go up in your head and you should try to change." As soon as he said "red flag," all the Americans in the audience started laughing. I'm not sure how that got translated. Talk about politically incorrect!

The former Soviet flag is, of course, what the audience had in mind.

Uphill Battle

A week after I'd bragged that ours is the only mission in the former Soviet Union and all of Eastern Europe that has not been plagued by religious and related political discrimination, enemies of the Church in Vyborg blocked our ground-breaking ceremony for the first Church property in all of Russia. However, chances are we may end up with an even more desirable piece of property. The city fathers try to mollify us, for they know we had every legal right to the project and would beat them if we took legal action. We won't take them to court, however, because we would surely win the battle but lose the war. Although the earlier project was a three-and-a-half-year undertaking, more patience is clearly called for.

Keys

With as many as two-thirds of our recently converted male members presently inactive, we must do more in terms of retention and reactivation. Two keys to increased Church growth are the number of active Melchizedek Priesthood holders and the effectiveness of branch presidents—hence my charge to help train them.

Courtesy Chris James

Graffiti on street corner. The spray-painted message, "Get rid of the Mormons," exemplifies the public opposition the Church often faces in the St. Petersburg area.

Spiritual Rearmament

Because of the harsh conditions of life here for so many, few have the luxury of being nearly so comfortable or complacent as we are in the West. Therefore, the emotional, psychological, and spiritual options are more readily apparent. Either they can opt for despair, cynicism, and utter moral default. Or they can choose the profound purpose for living afforded by the gospel and make the best of what they have. So, while it is much easier to attract people to our message and to convert them than, say, in western Europe, it is also harder for many to stay actively involved. After the glamour wears off and the need arises to be consistently there and ever willing to serve in mundane ways, the same familiar pressures and temptations to escape—alcohol being one of the foremost—may again sway them. Elder Max Caldwell of our Area Presidency discussed the matter with me just yesterday on the phone. He pointed out that the common scriptural injunction to "nourish" oneself spiritually, not just rely on *others* to sustain us, is one of the principles we do not teach well enough to investigators and new members.

"Jaked" again. Elder David Miller leaves a message for contacts after a thirteen-story climb to their apartment. Missionaries often deal with rejection and disappointment.

Reassurance

We've had to reconcile the missionaries to giving their best effort and being satisfied with whatever the results may be. They should not blame themselves but still be willing to do all they can. I think they are beginning to perceive that this is how they need to view their missions. They must not feel that results as such are totally up to them. They need to realize that there are still many potential golden converts out there as admirable and promising as our wonderful members.

I think the missionaries are learning to view their circumstances more in that fashion. In fact, I recently requested that as two of the Brethren (a Seventy and an Apostle) address our missionaries, they encourage and reassure the missionaries about themselves. Both leaders were very perceptive in that regard and avoided putting their audience on a guilt trip or making them feel they weren't working as they needed to. Instead, the speakers helped the missionaries better understand that their efforts are meaningful and that to be assured of this they need to trust the Lord. Elder Dallin H. Oaks extensively used the expression "trust" in connection with faith and the significance of missionary activity irrespective of visible results.

Fine Line

The line dividing serious emotional impairment or circumstantial victimization from plain character weakness or a bad attitude is sometimes mighty thin and terribly hard to discern.

Palpable

From Elder Anthony Wilding:

> Elder Jonathan McKinnon and I have been in our area now for three weeks and it has been hard to keep going. Since the small group we are tending is only about two months old and there are no members as yet, the talks and needs of the meetings fall entirely on the missionaries. Since there are only four of us, I've had many opportunities to speak and teach in Russian, and although it's tough, I've learned a lot. In addition, while the people are friendly and pleased to help, they are slow to accept the gospel.

> We did meet a great guy the other day and were able to teach him a first discussion. I felt it had gone about like most others. But when we went back for a second discussion, the man mentioned that

while reading in the book we'd given him he'd come to a passage he wanted us to explain further. We were both quite stunned. Then he opened it to Moroni 10 and started reading verses 3 through 5. As we talked with him about Moroni's promise, the feeling in the room was as warm as a feather comforter and made us feel just as secure.

Just then I happened to look into the man's eyes and saw what can only be called a radiant light. The Spirit had filled this man's mind with understanding and belief in the Lord's powerful promise. No matter where I go or what I do up ahead, I will never forget the moment when I saw the Spirit settle upon one of our Heavenly Father's children.

Pomp and Pageantry

Each spring Merriam and I have missed Russian Orthodoxy's most grandiose celebration—its Easter service, something we'd always intended to take in. But we are less entranced these days by such pageantry and display than we were in premission days. Besides, the service culminates at midnight, and each time we've been just too exhausted.

Reciprocal

To be here under these circumstances, to witness the response of many wonderful persons who never even knew Christ until recently, and to have the gospel "take" so thoroughly with them is truly inspiring (despite some rather dismal statistics regarding the membership in general). That response is a profound witness of the restored gospel's universal relevance and importance for all people. Understandably, such persons also emerge as our finest leaders. And there are quite a few young people who are like this too.

By their example, all of them have made the gospel and the Church all the more significant and meaningful in our and other missionaries' lives. We are impelled to emulate them and to reflect the same commitment. That's probably the greatest reward for just being willing to serve—that what you thought you were bringing to others comes back to you, many fold. I'm reminded of this statement in a CNN interview by Bishop Desmond Tutu, the South African Anglican bishop and Nobel Peace Prize winner: "We went to the ghetto to minister to them, but instead they ministered to us." We have experienced in St. Petersburg what he did in Johannesburg.

Year Three

Summer 1995
to
Spring 1996

Faith Affirmed: Summer 1995

Question

Vyacheslav Kondratev, now our senior district president, recently asked me, "What are your greatest impressions since coming here?" I managed to answer, "Faith and love. Love and faith." And the way things seem to fall apart on at least a weekly basis before they're somehow put back together. The momentary crises that seem so devastating but always somehow get resolved with our mutual effort and the transcendent guidance we at first don't think to call on. Our general failure to recognize that others are more faithful and enduring than we give them credit for.

Nephite Disease

What hampers conversion is not so much people's reservations about the message itself. Skeptics probably won't talk to the missionaries in the first place. It's mostly a complacency about what they've settled for in their lives—not caring to stop smoking or drinking or to marry the person they're living with. It's self-indulgence. What we are calling them to repent of is not significant enough to them to abandon.

When things were harder and less reassuring just a year ago—when people couldn't be sure what the future held for them (not that they can do so even now), when goods were less accessible—they were more humble and desperate. Then they were more willing to change in order to have the consolation and the reassurance with which a spiritual life would richly compensate them.

A Royal Army

One of Merriam's short but inspired addresses to the missionaries:

Dear elders and sisters of the Russia, Saint Petersburg Mission!

After this past week, with the wonderful *prazdnik* [holiday] that celebrated the fifty-year anniversary of the end of the Second World War, my mind has been riveted on thoughts of armies. You missionaries are also an army.

National pastime. Many Russians turn to liquor to escape feelings of depression. Addiction to alcohol can then hamper conversion. Elder Loren Hulse stands in front of graffiti, which is often written in English, the most fashionable post-Soviet foreign language.

Your army does not battle with bullets because you are warriors of the Word. You do not inflict fear and confusion, but through understanding of this precious Word, you bring stability and hope.

Your army does not search and destroy but finds and saves. You are not only soldiers of salvation but ambassadors of amnesty—leaving in your wake new hope for the future. Your army does not imprison because you are liberators of the soul.

As you move through your assigned areas, you bring no death, misery, or destruction. Instead you offer peace to the world and to individual human hearts.

You valiant sons and daughters of God, who live true to the promise you made in your premortal life to so serve, I love and salute you. I thank God from the bottom of my heart for allowing me to march in your ranks.

Perestroika

We've been told that, ideally, we should try to have between 100 and 150 members in every branch before we consider splitting them. I think that's well advised. However, I don't think that means we can't still form smaller groups as well (groups are budding, unofficial local units comprised mostly of investigators). We've also recently been urged to consider merging branches that were once split off from one another, particularly where one of them is not growing well and its priesthood strength is very meager.

Just last night, in fact, we decided to request such a merger. The interesting thing is that the newer of the two branches, originally formed as a group of investigators on the territory of the older branch, is now

Courtesy Gail Halvorsen

Friends in the gospel. Dima Borisov *(left)*, a young convert and newly ordained elder from the small branch in Pushkin, was privileged to baptize his good friend Sergey Gribovsky.

the stronger of the two. So, by bringing them together, a kind of grafting procedure, you get an even stronger hybrid unit. This represents greater growth than would be possible by just staying with an original entity and trying to bring investigators to it. There's nothing lost, and everything to be gained.

Scale Helps

Larger gatherings of members, district- or missionwide, seem to have a particularly edifying effect. A sizable meeting of members or investigators—almost all of them so impressive to be around—helps allay an individual's doubt and fear about getting involved in something that might otherwise seem too strange and off-the-wall to justify its profound claims.

Incentive

As our members return from the Sweden Stockholm Temple—a party of twenty attends every second or third month—it becomes clear what an additional incentive the temple becomes in their lives and what a boost it is for the Church here. They all seem grateful and overwhelmed. Going to the temple commits people to take their membership more seriously. And it reassures them about their eternal relationship with their ancestors and with the deceased members of their immediate family. The sacrifices the Russian members must make to attend the temple further attests to their impressive faith and dedication.

Kaliningrad

This year, the final year of our call, we were privileged to receive the former East Prussian capital, Königsberg, now Kaliningrad, into our mission. We make our second trip there next week, flying across the Baltic countries to the former eastern reaches of Germany. The branch in Kaliningrad is probably our most *perspektivny* (promising) in terms of future growth. Most of the old German buildings are gone and have been replaced by crumbling, concrete monstrosities. In this regard, Kaliningrad resembles other Hanseatic ports like Gdańsk (the former Danzig) and Silesian cities like Wrocław (the former Breslau) in Poland.

During our first trip to Kaliningrad, we read an account of the LDS Church there in the 1920s (sent on by President Robert Blair from Riga). At that time, the city's several branches constituted some 840 German members, with a 120-member touring choir. Among the first missionaries to Kaliningrad was an East Prussian, the father of Richard Boehm, my first junior companion in the North German Mission (1956). Other early missionaries were a Liechty from Provo (our neighbor Ken's uncle) and Bill Hoskisson, another Provo neighbor and fellow ward member. Additionally, the late University of Utah art professor Charles Dibble, served back then as well, as did the fathers of both Elders Robert K. Dellenbach and Dennis B. Neuenschwander of our Area Presidency.

Those missionaries were persecuted by the Kaiser's government far more than ours thus far in Russia—they were jailed, deported, and so forth. Offsetting the Church's impressive beginnings at the time were excommunications, defections to the Josephites (Reorganized Church), and harassment by former members, who on at least one occasion pelted the missionaries with orange peels and eggs. So we really don't have it so bad after all. [By 1999 there were two branches in Kaliningrad, totaling over 200 members.]

Fundamental Concepts

In a calling like this, one is inclined to consider more often than usual what is truly instructive about the restored gospel—what is otherwise not known or available to those we teach. Three fundamental concepts keep recurring to my mind:

- the spiritual nature of all that is earthly or material—for example, our bodies and the Earth itself
- the divine heritage and potential of all human beings
- the eternal nature of families.

[This overall impression would be confirmed by that of a non-LDS scholar, John L. Brooke, in *The Refiner's Fire: The Making of Mormon Cosmology, 1644–1844* (Cambridge University Press, 1994), which I read after returning from our mission.]

Pioneers

I've underestimated three people. One is the first native Russian missionary to serve in the United States. Looking much like Harpo Marx, he showed up one morning in my office to be released. The other two are a semiactive couple who are always at conferences to greet the visiting seventies but who seem to feel slighted that they are not basically running the mission.

All three played key roles at the outset. The missionary was a charter member of the Church in Russia and the very first to be baptized on Russian soil since before the Revolution. The married couple were the first Soviet citizens ever to join the Church (baptized in Hungary). Their St. Petersburg apartment was the site of the first gathering of members in Russia. Here I've been rubbing shoulders with these remarkable pioneers and, because of their rough edges, failed to appreciate their earlier critical contributions. [The former missionary, Anton Skripko, is presently serving as the St. Petersburg Mission's first native seminary and institute coordinator. Another noteworthy first for Brother Anton.]

Déjà Vu

For most of my life, I did not understand the term *déjà vu*. Perhaps the concept itself could make sense only after a form of it was vividly experienced. In July one such event involved the unexpected deaths of two relatively young, very devout members. What in retrospect so impacted me was an event involving both of them during a prior conference of their district. While presiding as a member of the district presidency, one of these two members, Brother L, cast aspersions on an absent branch president, suggesting that the branch president's nonattendance was a sin. It was clearly an unfortunate remark and not the first time Brother L had, in his particularly zealous manner, proved either harshly judgmental or extremely presumptuous. I tried to put the moment's awkwardness out of my mind, hoping that others would too.

In the second hour, the other devout member, who was the district Young Men's president, passed a note my way, asking if he could bear testimony—again an irregular sort of initiative in any Church meeting. But, for some reason, I invited him to come forward after the next speaker—which he then did. His testimony though, if that is what it was, proved as unusual as his request. What he did, calmly and courteously I'm glad to say, was to chastise Brother L for maligning another person in a public meeting. He said what I would have wanted to say later, in private. L seemed to take it in stride, and nothing more was said. I was as much intrigued by it all as I was slightly dismayed.

I was even more dismayed when both men passed away shortly after— L from a brain tumor and the youth leader after falling from a roof he'd climbed on to watch fireworks during a public holiday. Who could have foreseen on the day of the conference that neither would be with us much longer? Death recalled for us their remarkable devotion to their callings and just how much we loved and now truly missed them, despite their personal idiosyncrasies.

How in the mission field does one more fully perceive both one's self and fellow members? Much the way our Creator does, as both flawed and precious. How, at home, do we more often tend to view one another and sometimes ourselves? As less flawed—and also less precious.

Kaddish—Lament for the Dead

Yesterday we attended L's funeral at the crematorium we visited over a year ago. L was only in his forties and was both our mission genealogy leader and a counselor in a district presidency. He was earlier an extremely knowledgeable and enthusiastic Sunday School and institute teacher. No one was ever more committed, more focused. But two weeks before his unexpected death, others—mostly sisters—came to me expressing their dismay that he had been called to assist in the temple. They complained about the personal advice they had not asked for, the admonitions, the implied censure, the tendency to dispute small points of doctrine, the assertion of his titles when presiding, his insistence on the superiority of his Jewish bloodline, the need to be recognized as others' patriarch and priesthood advisor (even when he wasn't), his personal history of four unsuccessful marriages prior to joining the Church, and his former wives, who did all they could to keep their whereabouts unknown to him.

What the sisters complained of did not surprise me. L had aggravated me often enough too—and worried me about the impression he made on others as a Church officer. But he had managed to do us all this favor—before the next temple trip, before people could feel further harassed and complain some more, he died. In doing so, he also gave each of us pause to consider whether, in his case, we should have taken the higher road more often. Many felt bad about the way they had resented him so.

On the whole, L's funeral was easier to take than Vladislav's a year ago. Perhaps we knew this time what to expect. L's last wife was there too. I'd been told he had introduced her to the Church, but as far as I know she had been inactive since their divorce. She couldn't have been more than eighteen when they married, just half his age, the one we were told he had beaten. She sobbed throughout. She must have still loved him.

L was clothed in the temple attire we'd managed to have a missionary's parents bring over with them just in time. And his silent and rather nondescript father, an ethnic Jew who, we understood, was not a believer, at the last moment threw himself on the bier and wept with abandon, calling out, "My son! My son!" At that moment, I envied L. Nor did I want to inquire if the Church approves cremation of a corpse dressed in temple garb. Or if the morticians disrobe corpses first. And, if so, do we get the clothing back. I don't think I will inquire either, unless there are other such instances while we are here. I know that L, particularly, would have wanted it that way. He was a man, someone said, who had never known any happiness, but he had demonstrated great hope, faith, and dedication during his two and a half years as a member, particularly with respect to the temple. Those few last years were a meaningful compensation.

And we saw him mellow. The sister who had during his last two weeks so devotedly nursed L—she also has Jewish antecedents—had in turn fallen in love with him. She will succeed him as mission genealogy leader and would like nothing better than to be sealed to him, which we told her could happen only in the life to come if both are willing.

As I think again about the service that preceded L's cremation and the quick destruction of his garb and remains in an oven before we'd even departed, I was somehow reminded of the "strike" in which a play's stage set is reduced to as close to ashes as possible. I've often felt that theater is such an ephemeral art. But so is mortality—extremely ephemeral.

A sad echo of earlier events—the son about to be cremated, the distraught father, both Jews.

A Glass Darkly

I increasingly sense the role of circumstances in others' lives. Many things are not in their control, even though a sense of personal accountability and belief in one's agency can in *most* instances make a considerable difference. Still, I am constrained from being quite so judgmental.

Rationale

It is perhaps necessary that unfit parents bear children and innocent people become the victims of abuse, that there be genocide, that after the deaths of the first Apostles there was an apostasy, and that the missionaries' message be so frequently rejected. Free agency is just that inviolable.

Amazing Grace

President Evgeny Katz of the Obukhovsky Branch, another member of Jewish descent, recently shared with us an amazing encounter with old friends who had emigrated to Colorado about two years ago. They were here for the holidays to visit their families, and he just happened to meet them again on Nevsky Prospekt. Though friends of his, these were people whose interests and whose very personalities had, in Katz's view, been totally mercenary. Earlier they had shown no interest in ideas, and when they talked about books, it was only in terms of a book's price and the profit one could make from it.

But as they spoke with him this time, they amazed President Katz by asking how he felt about

Courtesy Gail Halvorsen

Evgeny Katz. Katz, an outstanding musician, actor, and philosopher as well as lawyer, is legally blind. Of Jewish descent—his grandfather was a rabbi—he presided over one of the St. Petersburg branches.

112

Jesus Christ. He assured them that his personal relationship with Christ was quite positive. They then asked him if he knew that the true church of Christ was present and available in the United States. He answered affirmatively. The questioning continued until they mentioned the Book of Mormon. He then told them that he too had read it. Then his friends told him that, although they had not yet joined The Church of Jesus Christ of Latter-day Saints, they'd been attending services and had even paid tithing for a full year. They were in turn equally amazed to learn that the Church is in Russia and (*coup de grace*) that their old friend is not only a member but the leader of one of several congregations here in their hometown.

President Katz is sure they will join the Church when they return to Colorado but added that they are the last acquaintances to whom he would have ever referred the missionaries. He was dumbfounded about the way they've responded to the gospel and the extent to which it has already changed them.

Good Samaritan

From Elder Brett Johnson:

After serving the first three weeks of my mission in Vilnius, Lithuania, I was informed I would be transferred to Kaliningrad, Russia. One of my greatest fears in being transferred to Kaliningrad was that I would have to cross the border. I knew all of the horror stories of missionaries being harassed by border guards, and now I was supposed to cross the Lithuanian-Russian border by myself with three weeks of missionary work under my belt.

My companion, Elder Aleksandr Bazarsky, put me on the bus in the early afternoon. I took a seat next to the window and after a few minutes was joined by a Russian girl of about fifteen. Not knowing enough Russian to really make conversation and being scared to death of the trip's outcome, I sat quietly in my seat and stared out the window. Thoughts of being dragged off the bus played in my mind. Meanwhile, the girl next to me spent the four-hour trip to the border visiting with what seemed to be her mother and brother and reading an Orthodox prayer book.

Before I knew it, we had reached the border. A Russian guard got on board and told us to exit the bus. We all did so and formed a line leading to a one way mirrored booth where they were checking passports and visas. As we stood in line, the guard asked the bus driver about certain suitcases in the luggage compartment under the bus. The driver pointed at me, and the guard slowly came my way. He asked (I assume) about my suitcases, and almost in unison, the other passengers told him I didn't speak Russian. One lady told me in broken English that he wanted to look through my bags. I pretended not to understand (which wasn't entirely an act). The pretense seemed to work—he just closed the luggage compartment without rummaging through my personal belongings.

It was soon my turn to show my papers to the guard at the booth. He took my passport and said something in Russian. Again, everyone told him I didn't understand the language. The next thing I knew, another guard escorted me back onto the bus without my passport. One by one, the others also returned to the bus, except, I noticed, each of them was carrying his passport. The bus was soon full again, and the driver started the motor. I completely panicked, but before I could do anything, the girl sitting next to me ran to the front of the bus and told the driver to stop. We waited for a moment, and then a guard boarded the bus and returned my passport. I breathed a sigh of relief.

Shortly after we passed into Russia, the girl and her family got off. All I could say was *spasibo* [thank you]. She smiled and left. An Orthodox girl had helped out a Mormon missionary. At this point, I understood the story of the good Samaritan and fell in love with the Russian people. This girl, whose name I didn't even know, performed what was to me one of the most charitable acts I'd ever witnessed. It was a simple thing, but it was just what Christ would have done. The spirit I then felt stayed with me all the way to Kaliningrad.

Mormon Arts

For the BYU Singers' concert, we managed to fill the former imperial concert hall, the Kapella (just across Palace Square from the Hermitage), with an audience of nearly nine hundred. Such numbers are practically unheard of these days, however spectacular the artists who perform there each evening in a different program. This was, of course, not the audience that would normally attend there. The majority were our members and investigators, few of whom are serious patrons of the arts. But what better way to bring high culture to the masses than through the Church itself. (For many, this concert was not just a "leveler" but a "heightener," an enhancement of taste and aesthetic experience.) How ironic that we could induce only half that number to return the next week to hear Elder Oaks. Yes, music is a great and powerful medium.

[The following spring, we filled another hall with 1,200 spectators to witness the remarkable BYU Folk Dancers. A local choreographer insisted they were better than Russia's most celebrated folk dance troupe, the Moiseev Dancers. All of the BYU performers are only amateurs, but like the missionaries, they are on fire with a purpose beyond themselves.]

Good Riddance

There are always interesting new brushfires that make the time go particularly fast. Tourist season is almost over. We'll be less plagued by the occasional Old World "discoverer" who has all kinds of special demands and who instantly becomes an expert on the Church scene here for the fireside circuit back home.

Coping: Autumn 1995

Mother Russia

Again the remarkable Dostoevskian contrasts come together here between the sublime and the despicable, with hardly any pastels or shades of gray. The Russian condition vividly illustrates the contrasting states of spiritual life and spiritual death, as these in turn affect our personal relationships. How heart wrenching to counsel with members such as these:

- a former branch president and his wife, now separated and both adulterers
- the wife of another leader who has utterly alienated half their branch, a situation that will shortly necessitate his release
- the mother of a thirty-seven-year-old son, who still leaches off of her while regularly beating and reviling her—both are members.

Pride, unwillingness to admit one's own culpability, and spiritual stagnation so clearly lie behind each instance.

These stark circumstances lead me to believe I have found the icon typifying Russia in *Argumenty i fakty,* October 1995:

> Motherly Love: The small polar train station, Inta. I enter the waiting room. Dirt, spittle, cigarette butts, drunken faces. I look around. Where should I sit? Then I see a thin, exhausted old woman, her arms tucked into the sleeves of her coat and supporting an immense basket. Her head is bowed. It's hard to tell if she is sleeping, or crying. Then she raises her head and my heart stops: I've never seen such beauty in an older person—the deep blue of her eyes, her gray hair, the ruddy complexion beneath the network of wrinkles. I had never imagined that one could look so lovely at such an age. "Why are you staring at me, my dear?" "Grandmother, you're so beautiful." "I was as a child. It was God's gift. People couldn't take their eyes off me when I was young, and they still can't. But my beauty didn't bring me either happiness or fortune. Only tears and, yes, my love for my son. I'm traveling to the district prison to visit him. I'm not sure I'll find a shelter there, or if I'll hold out. But the love in my heart will." A deep sigh, and then tears come to her eyes. "Yes, I still have that love in my heart. Here. I'll show you." Slowly she unfolds her arms. Horror! Instead of hands there are two red stumps. "My son chopped them off with an axe. He was drunk and wanted money for vodka, but I had none."

116

Courtesy Wendy Bingham Stepan

Sister Wendy Bingham (Stepan) with Lyudmila Antipova, charter member of Vyborg Relief Society. At the time this picture was taken, Sister Antipova was eighty-six years old.

Jewish Happiness

Recently I persuaded our office elders to join me as spectators of something both silly and utterly endearing—a Jewish musical comedy produced by local Jewish thespians and entitled *Jewish Happiness (Yevreyskoe schaste)*—a euphemism for bad luck. It's an *Abie's Irish Rose*—set in Manhattan, about the social-financial rise and fall of Russian émigrés who are trying to marry off their eligible daughter. The audience was clearly made up of the remnant of St. Petersburg's Jewish community—those who haven't already gone abroad.

This frothy piece had such a hold on me for two reasons: The singing and dancing, the gestures and intonations, were so ethnically distinctive, so what I still imagine European Jewry to have been like. Additionally, those performing and those in the audience enjoyed their shared heritage and one another's company, reciprocally resonating their mutual fondness and camaraderie. Their interactions contrasted with those of many Russians and most Americans, even Mormons, who generally intermingle superficially.

We exited past the Theater of Comedy box office, where others were lining up for tickets to more standard Russian fare. I heard a few scoffs as they noticed the announcement of the specially scheduled performances of *Jewish Happiness.* "Your Jewish neighbors could show you a thing or two," I felt like saying to them. "Maybe that's why you've always disliked them so!"

Prognosis

A particular syndrome is observed in a very few missionaries. They are utterly disorganized, very hard on younger companions without knowing it, spacey, idealistic, good with people but afraid to contact strangers, neglectful of their health, truly charitable and lovable but utterly impractical, and, deep down, terribly insecure. The mission experience really does not seem to change them. How will they fare in a marriage or in the mean, cutthroat world? Much as they try to minister to others, they themselves need even more nurturing and probably always will. I doubt they will get it. Life will be hard for them.

Valiant

Fear of frequent rejection keeps most missionaries from thrusting in their sickle regularly and enthusiastically. Those who somehow break through that barrier enjoy much greater success, which in turn encourages them further. In this struggle, all are truly heroic—doing something that does not come easily for anyone. Their circumstance is like that of voyagers and crew on a vessel with a long passage and far destination—they cooperate, remain steady during unexpected storms, hold to the rudder, and still keep in mind their course and where it is meant to take them, having faith that it will do so.

"Heal Thyself"

One thing is certain: missionary companions need to confront one another, and I need to confront them too if certain festering differences are ever to be resolved. All of which must have prompted these words of mine in a recent mission bulletin:

> Surely one of the worst imaginable punishments and tortures is
> solitary confinement. Perhaps that is why the sons of perdition, about

whom we fortunately know so little, are to be consigned to outer darkness. But in some instances a kind of solitary confinement also occurs in the life of a missionary.

This happens, for example, when we emotionally hold back from our companion, priesthood leaders, or other mission associates. We may hold back by failing to share our real feelings (maybe in proselytizing too!), showing sufficient interest and appreciation, or being unwilling to offer or ask for help, which of course we all need. When we thus draw into ourselves, we consign our companion and others to the same lonely condition.

Such a response clearly contradicts both the spirit of the gospel we've been called to preach and the Lord's first two and greatest commandments. This withdrawal surely deprives us of the Spirit and renders us less effective. We are then also more strongly tempted to distract ourselves with other pursuits.

How we respond is ultimately a question of our dedication and desire to do better and to follow through. By humbling ourselves, each of us can know where we most need to improve. So, as we preach the gospel of repentance, we need, in the first order, to preach it to ourselves.

May we all better recognize that one of the Lord's great gifts to his full-time missionaries is a twenty-four-hour-a-day companion. Another gift is the challenge and need this companionship affords us to overcome our self-absorption, our self-pity, and our aversion or indifference to others who may not be like us or may see things differently. There is no more important training for or diagnostic testing of how successfully you will cope in your future marriage.

Miscast?

From Sister Jill Cherrington [now Christensen]:

When I moved into the Shuvalovsky Branch, the elders introduced my companion, Sister Saria Isokangas, and me to a woman they had met and started teaching. Her name is Nelly, and she had already been taught three discussions. She was very interested in the Church. Nelly is an amazing woman. When she first met the missionaries, she'd had a very hard life. She was very poor and living in a communal apartment, didn't have a job, was pregnant, had an abusive boyfriend, and until recently had a brother living with her who was an alcoholic. She also had very little food.

Since we've started teaching her, she has overcome a lot of her problems. She is reading the Book of Mormon and coming to church faithfully. Nelly is still extremely poor, with little or no food and without any income. She has given birth to a little girl who is malnourished and slightly underdeveloped because both she and Nelly are starving. Winter is coming quickly, and she doesn't have much warm clothing. Her apartment has a broken window with tape over the cracks and plastic taped in where there is no glass. In her tiny cold room, there is little or no furniture, all of which is breaking. All she has is art work from the children in her building, who adore her. Their pictures cover her walls.

In view of these circumstances, Sister Isokangas and I took a sister from the branch and her three-year-old son with us to teach her the fifth discussion about sacrifice. I was nervous to teach her about tithing and fast offerings because I knew that she literally had nothing and these would be difficult principles for her to accept.

It felt like Grand Central Station in her tiny room. Nelly has a friend named Sveta, who is usually drunk. Sveta has two sweet daughters, ages four and five, and they had come to be with us. So there we all were in this small room, talking about sacrifice: Sister Isokangas and I, the member and her small son, Nelly holding her baby daughter, and Sveta with her two girls. At the end of the discussion, we bore testimony about how important sacrifice is and how blessed we were for having sacrificed. I then asked Nelly, "Will you give ten percent of your income to the Lord after you are baptized?"

Just after I asked that question, Sveta, who was drunk, became angry at her youngest daughter and struck her very hard on the side of the head, causing her head to hit against the back of a chair. Thus the little girl received two hard blows. Of course, she started to cry and ran to Nelly for comfort. So here was Nelly with a baby in one arm and a crying girl in the other, with a room full of people staring at her and waiting to hear how she would answer. Nelly paused for a moment and took a deep breath. Then, with all the dignity and class imaginable, she turned to Sveta and pled with her to not hit her daughter. Then she turned to me and said, "Well, I know that tithing is a commandment, and I know that it is important for me to obey all the Lord's commandments. So, yes, I will."

Nelly has such a strong testimony of the gospel that she has a real glow about her. She knows the love of her Heavenly Father and radiates that love to others. She is so willing to do what is right that she would give anything she has, though she has so very little. What a humbling experience it has been for me, who has always been blessed with so many comforts, to waltz into Nelly's life and try to teach her what it means to sacrifice. It's really ironic that on this subject I should be the teacher and Nelly the student when it's really the other way around.

Dysfunction

I am regularly reminded of the consequences of dysfunctional homes. Some missionaries have such inordinate trouble adjusting. My sense is these individuals come from a family background reflecting either extreme neglect or both over-indulgent and unusually demanding parental expectations, such as, "You are better than everyone else," and, "You'd better not disappoint me!" As I wrote in a later bulletin, I hope not too unkindly:

> Under the very real pressures of a mission—and later, of course, marriage—psychologists tell us we tend to respond in our relationships as we were conditioned to in our youth. When stressed, we react in the same immature and less-than-ideal ways that we did toward our perhaps less-than-ideal parents and siblings. As we all know, there are fewer ideal—nonbroken or nondysfunctional—families in today's world, even in Zion. And, when this is so, everyone to some degree becomes a victim.
>
> My heart goes out to those of you with such personal backgrounds. I see, I believe, how in many instances it has adversely affected you. But with the Lord's and his servants' help, anyone can be healed with time and effort and sincere intent. That is after all his promise and the promise of his gospel, which we preach: "Physician, heal thyself."

Perplexed

My biggest bane just now is a missionary (one of very few during our time here) who thoroughly frustrates me. He is one that neither I nor anyone else can seem to break through to. He is utterly, condescendingly misanthropic, totally condemning of and constantly complaining about the other missionaries and anything we do that goes even slightly wrong or that does not garner his approval, which is almost everything any of us do. Emotionally stunted, he flinches at an embrace and rejects anyone's attempt to say, "I love you."

On top of it all, he is extremely intelligent. Perhaps having superior intelligence is the reason some Mormons are so unteachable and so certain of themselves and why they "know" in all instances so much better than anyone else. Scriptural admonitions about humility, "a contrite spirit," and submissiveness go unheeded.

Missionary Types

My perception of various departing missionaries at the airport gate: Some make sure they are seen off by a sizable retinue of fans, mostly female. Others, at all costs, avoid telling either members or investigators the particulars of their departure—they prefer to slip quietly away. They are the more committed missionaries who managed to get sufficiently outside themselves. The criteria for their achievement did not include popularity.

My insightful assistant suggests that missionaries come in three categories: those who are fully, internally motivated; those who ploddingly, dutifully go through the motions; and

Courtesy Chad Smith

A "bad day" at the mission office. A mission president is often a surrogate father for elders and sisters under his direction and must cope with their sense of humor.

those who have particular difficulty fulfilling what they were called here to accomplish. Very wisely, my assistant adds that from time to time we are each one of these three.

"Being There"

I just saw off two more elders who have ended their missions—lifelong friends from the same posh U.S. suburb. They were generally viewed by other missionaries as charismatic goldbrickers, who, if they never strained themselves, at least held out. However, as we heard their testimonies the night before they left, I was convinced of their lack of pretentiousness or false piety and of their basic loyalty and goodness.

I cannot afford to dismiss or underestimate anyone in our mission but must be there for all of them however much they may exasperate us or disapprove of one another. In other words, I must love everyone unconditionally, while firmly holding at bay requests for special favors that would exploit the Church's resources, give some an unfair advantage, or simply be unwise and not for their good.

Analogies

My assistant, Elder David Dayton, has been sharing with the missionaries the proselytizing analogy of how boiling water becomes steam at 212 degrees Fahrenheit. Crossing that energy threshold makes a difference in moving objects and propelling vehicles. An earlier assistant, Elder Grant Beckwith, used to talk about the energy required to propel rockets and space vehicles until they reach the state of zero gravity, where they then perform in a seemingly miraculous manner and appear to navigate almost effortlessly. Terms like *synergy, critical mass,* and *exponential growth*—each of which reflects real events in nature and human affairs—connote this same *momentum,* where things happen in wondrous ways and on an extraordinary scale.

Other great analogies proposed by former assistants (I wish I had kept a running list of them) include Elder Jayson Branch's allusion to the principle of "ordering up," which he had observed while serving customers at McDonald's. He always tried to encourage them to consider a complete meal—large fries, a shake, and a Big Mac instead of just a plain hamburger. Similarly, missionaries need to convey to those they meet the "big picture." For example: "As I look at you, I see a righteous family head who can literally help save his wife and children, his ancestors, and many other Russians."

Then there's Elder John Rather's haunting reference to the cat that runs across the stage at the Marinsky Theater—invariably during a tender, soulful moment such as a soloist's aria. Some audience members gasp, some titter, some even cry. Turning on one such occasion to the woman sitting next to him, Elder Rather asked, "Why is that cat there?" The answer: "We don't know. It just has to be." So it is with the presence of the Church in Russia, he suggested. Seeing us here, some gasp, some titter, some cry. Others become enraged. But it "has to be." It just "has to be."

More Missionary Responses

The first response is from a Russian, Elder Andrey Levashov, whose disappointment over the generally tepid reaction of his fellow countrymen reveals his own exceptional large-heartedness and other-directed idealism:

> After my first day of contacting I wept. Now I feel even more deeply the bottomless pit of dark ignorance and selfishness. People are inclined to exchange the Great Light for useless fragments of broken glass, while they remain in a state of fear and desperation. Even so, I can see glimmerings of hope for their emancipation.

And then the response from our Swede, Elder Johan Hallden—most telling in view of the general impression that Swedes tend to be reserved and unfriendly toward strangers, if not also toward one another:

> I'm sure you heard about the ferry boat that capsized going from Estonia to Stockholm. It happened during the night and very few survived. 800–900 passengers perished. The illegal workers were not on the lists and none of the children were counted either. My Mom wrote that all of Sweden grieved with the struck families and relatives. A friendship *never* there before was seen on the streets of Stockholm. On the buses and subways people—total strangers—were talking about life. The churches (all churches) were filled with people seeking God. As I read this my heart burst with happiness, and I could not hold back tears of gratitude and joy. Finally! Finally! My people are waking up. Finally.

And from a sister missionary, Wendy Bingham [Stepan]:

> We just returned from an appointment with an investigator who has complex problems, including bouts of severe depression. Tonight the subject turned to the Atonement of Christ. I testified to her that Jesus Christ understands her pain, anguish, trials, and every emotion because he *experienced* them. She answered a little bitterly that he *couldn't* understand because His suffering was for three days only, and besides He was *God*. The suffering was nothing to Him. Even as I then told her, "*Kazhdy raz, kogda Vam bol'no ili Vy stradaete, Emu bol'no i on stradaet!*" ("Every time you hurt or suffer, He hurts and suffers"), I knew it was true that Christ's suffering cannot end while humankind still suffers. She was quiet and thoughtful: "I just want Him to come sit with me for a while to tell me that He loves me and that everything will be all right." Then suddenly I knew that He *was* sitting there with her. He *was* telling her He loved her. He was there through *us*. I told her that, and she understood. *That's* what it means to "be on the Lord's errand." What an incredible work we are called to do!

Miracles of Consecration

Miracles can take place on a personal plane. As missionaries acquire and then maintain a steady focus on the work and on others, fear, self-doubt, sluggish indecisiveness, the misery of various forms of escape, and the struggle with self-control all seem to jettison and disappear. At that point, unexpected miracles begin to happen in the work itself. That's at least the testimony of those who have paid the price of total consecration. Nevertheless, we too often deny ourselves similar blessings: "That's just how they are, but I'm not like that."

International branch baptism. Despite the opposition, many willing individuals continue to search for and accept the truth. Miracles can occur. Elder Ray Banks *(fourth from right)* and Sister Pat Banks *(rear, far left)* with other missionaries and members of the St. Petersburg International Branch.

Carry On!

From Roderic Buttimore, an older missionary from Great Britain:

We had a rather sad experience at the end of this week. An investigator's wife passed me a letter, in which he wrote, "After considerable thought I have decided that my way of life won't allow me to meet with you any more or be baptized. I ask your pardon for the time you have wasted on me." It occurred to me, though he didn't know it, that this is a ridiculously pathetic statement. I am still hopeful that we can work with him.

I don't know what concerns he has, but why do I say that his statement is ridiculous? Because I could have used this excuse myself. I think the only one of the ten commandments I wasn't in violation of when I first met the missionaries was "Thou shalt not kill." I could easily have said, like this young man, "My lifestyle doesn't allow me to meet with you."

However, unlike him, I realized that I had to follow God and not run away from my responsibilities. Perhaps for me the miracle was not like Alma's or Paul's, but it was a miracle nonetheless. I've heard these words before. They are the words of the enemy of all righteousness, who knows that if he can take away people's hope, he can take away their freedom. Many times I have felt beyond redemption as I have struggled with the sins that controlled my life. But, luckily, I realized something that was the reason for my wanting to serve a mission.

One is never beyond redemption until one stops trying. In the words of one General Authority: "It matters not if you try and fail and try and fail again. It matters greatly if you try and fail and fail to try again." There is always hope, and I'm still trying. I don't know if I'll be a great missionary—in fact, I don't care, as long as I am trying to be one. I trust I will be able to carry this one piece of knowledge to those members and investigators who feel they have lost hope.

Spiritual Pain

From Elder Joshua Gardner, another older missionary:

I had a pretty intense emotional experience this week. We met with a veteran (almost my age) of the Afghanistan War for a first discussion. He is crippled and obviously struggling to deal with the changes in his life. He has been writing a Vietnam vet for support. He seemed like a guy who had his life and emotions "together" but was struggling under a huge weight. Even when he laughed or smiled, his face could not conceal his pain, and my heart about broke as I sat there. I don't think I could react so positively under those same conditions. Meeting him has left me with a lot of acutely felt emotions, not all of them "bad." I've been carrying them around for a few days and have thought a lot about him. I really hope that we can help him, heal him even (emotionally) with what we have to teach. Helping him would make everything worthwhile.

"What Did We Accomplish?"

Today we're sending back our first missionary to insist on returning home before the end of his time here. He was in Russia just three months, never caught the spirit of the work, hated it, could think only of his own convenience, and pretended his family needed him. (Now I'm almost glad he had that for an excuse.) He called the missionary rules "garbage." We all looked on with dismay as he flaunted them. At the airport, I'll tell him to have a good life and remind him that there've been plenty of others, even Apostles (including President Hunter) who never served missions—in case that will help him later.

We'll be sending back five others at the same time who went full term and who met with us just last night in an inspiring "debriefing" session. To the question "What did you accomplish here?" each answered, "Nothing. I did nothing really. I was just here, trying to encourage some others. But they did it all, with the Lord's help. I am nothing." I thought then of King Benjamin's sermon as well as Moses' reply to the Lord: "I know that man is nothing, which thing I never had supposed" (Moses 1:10). It then occurred to me that such utter self-abnegation is very cleansing and not at all bad.

These same outstanding missionaries also spoke of the opposition that had in fact been so spiritually strengthening: "It was very hard—the hardest thing I ever did." To the question "Which Russians do you admire most?" one answered, "Those who rejected our message. They forced me to consider it more seriously and think it through—which led to an even greater conviction on my part." Another: "All those drunks." Yet another: "One preparation day my companion and I were visiting one of the city's large cathedrals. We were the only ones there until a man came running past us, fell on his knees in the middle of the cathedral, and wept. That Russian inspired me more than anyone else." Still another asserted about his future life: "I won't easily give up what was so hard to achieve here."

I thought of the contrast of a local American anti-Mormon agitator. While trying to dissuade one of our missionaries, the man had said to a particular elder, "I prefer a religion where I can be comfortable feeling good about myself"—as if the Savior had ever admonished, "Go forth and be comfortable."

Striking Profile

I wrote the following about five of our most outstanding missionary leaders when asked to assess them:

> One of the brightest spirits I have ever known. Was absolutely *never* discouraged or lacked enthusiasm. Tearfully testified of feeling the Spirit. His motto—"Learn to love the hard things." Inspired *everyone*, buoyed up the most difficult companions.

> Cheerful and loving all to the very end of his mission. I thought of him as "The Beloved." A humble, inspiring assistant to the president and at the end of his mission the excited leader of a small group of members that grew and grew.

Had the distinction of being a junior companion longer than anyone in the mission—seventeen months—which is strictly circumstantial. In that same period he was a most caring and loving branch president and willingly learned the intricacies of mission finances just to train a new office couple. Extremely self-effacing, never complaining, soft spoken, an inspiration and peacemaker to all.

Enthusiasm personified. One of our hardest-working proselytizers, cheerful and enthusiastic at every turn. A whole group of members fell in love with him as their leader and later became one of our strongest, most close-knit branches. Not very articulate, but radiating the Spirit and dedication from every pore.

A totally committed proselytizing elder who also deeply endeared himself to the branch he served as president. Inspired a more serious application in other missionaries. Felt the Spirit deeply, tearfully. Reflected quiet dignity. His motto—"The best missionary is a repenting missionary." We still quote him.

And there were others. Note how each description emphasizes (a) a consistently positive outlook and (b) a deeply felt companionship with the Spirit. Both seem to go hand in hand. Those who exemplified these qualities so noticeably were not typical, and their being so did not come easily or automatically. These missionaries worked at it because of their total submission to the Lord's work. Their willingness was in turn a consequence of their personal faith, commitment, and dedication. I pray I may keep that same trusting, positive spirit as I fade into physical decrepitude.

Onward and Upward: Winter 1996

Cosmic Connection

For me there's an especially memorable work by Chekhov called "The Student," his only short story I would characterize as having a transcendent spiritual dimension. On our last Christmas Day in Russia, I shared "The Student" with our current contingent of 130 missionaries.

The story takes place during the cold, still, dark days before Easter (not unlike the December we were presently facing). Returning to his village home, a young seminarian stops to warm himself at a fire tended by two destitute peasant women, a mother and daughter, who are both widows. He recalls for them the account of Peter's denial of Christ, whose setting is a fire on a similar dark, cold night. As he does so, the women, who sense the Savior's loneliness and travail more deeply than the student, begin to weep. Their response triggers in the young man the recognition that he, the women, and the people in the Bible account all share the same travail and, with unexpected joy, he feels one with them and with all creation:

Courtesy J. Preston Hughes

He thought that truth and beauty, which had guided human life there in the garden and in the yard of the high priest, had continued without interruption to this day and had evidently always been the chief thing in human life and in all earthly life, indeed; and the feeling of youth, health, vigor—he was only twenty-two—and the inexpressible sweet expectation of happiness, of

Elder Jesualdo Condori and his Savior. A rare Russian-speaking missionary from Lima, Peru, Elder Condori was called to serve in the Russia St. Petersburg Mission following his studies at Rostov.

> unknown mysterious happiness, took possession of him little by little, and life seemed to him enchanting, marvelous, and full of lofty meaning. (*The Chekhov Omnibus: Selected Stories*, trans. Constance Garnett, ed. Donald Rayfield [1994], 298)

As I read, I could hardly get through it. Without saying more, I hoped the missionaries could sense how much like the young seminarian they are and how much self-understanding their investigators' faith and appreciation of the gospel message brings to the missionaries.

Since then I've thought more and more about the story's many implications—particularly about our contemplation of others' spiritual frailty and consequent sorrow (as with Peter's denial of the Savior). Such fellow feeling both humbles and unites us with one another, affording unexpected joy together with a renewed sense of wonder about life itself. This process seems a fair description of how the gospel works.

Healing Faith

From Elder Alma Perry:

> As you know, we have been traveling down from Vyborg to a neighboring village to teach a wonderful family. This week, in tears, the mother called us to say her three daughters were extremely ill. She wanted to know if someone could come there and give them a blessing. My companion and I said we would stop by. The trip involved an hour's travel time by train and a thirty-minute walk through three feet of snow in the middle of a forest.

> When we finally arrived and explained the importance of blessings, I was amazed at the young girls' great faith. All three were blessed that they would speedily recover from an illness that had already lasted several weeks. The very next day, all were doing well, especially the youngest, who was outside playing when we stopped back as we had promised. I have never seen such faith in action.

[A month later, the two older girls were baptized, and their mother committed to do the same.]

Ordeal

Our one hospitalization of a missionary here (in lieu of evacuating him to Finland or somewhere else in the West, as we had in the past): on a weekend, Elder Robert Brunt came down with symptoms of appendicitis. The attending physician also diagnosed pneumonia. Off we sent him to one of St. Petersburg's most elite hospitals.

Unfortunately, its procedures, we soon discovered, were no better than they are most everywhere. Elder Brunt was not given the sophisticated tests that would verify appendicitis before an appendectomy, nor was the organ tested after its removal. The initial recovery, which lasted three days, was in an open ward where hypodermic needles may have had random and repeated use. Nor were any of us permitted to make contact with the elder until days later when he was brought to the hospital's modern recovery wing. (A less-hardy patient might well have gone bonkers!)

After that, the doctor in charge insisted on treating the elder for his pneumonia with massive shots of an antibiotic that could induce permanent deafness as well as kidney failure if the medication is not properly monitored. (We learned this only when we identified it and consulted with Elder Brunt's father, who is a physician.) Elder Brunt's ears were already popping, but the doctor refused to forego the shots and insisted he remain in the hospital for an indefinite number of days.

We took the matter into our own hands and shortly spirited him away when the doctor wasn't there. Elder Brunt recovered fully, and we will never know if he really had appendicitis, whose symptoms, we learned, are sometimes imitated by those of pneumonia. So now, as earlier, we tend to refer ailing missionaries to a Western clinic, the American Medical Center, which charges over $200 for the first visit.

When You Least Expect

From Elder Troy Peterson:

You may remember that Elder Daniel Robrecht and I are teaching a woman named Natasha. Her husband is very supportive but uninterested in our message. Natasha is a great investigator, though. She always fulfills her commitments and is making great progress. She reads the Book of Mormon regularly and attends church faithfully. Just one thing stands in her way—she's been afraid to pray. We've read verses about prayer, talked about what to say in a prayer, and tried to help her resolve her fears about praying.

This week, at long last, she decided she was ready to pray with us. Every time we've met with her, we've asked if she would like to pray at the end of the discussion. She's declined so many times that I almost didn't notice when on this occasion she said, "Yes." I was about to say the prayer myself when she stopped me and said, "I am ready to pray."

As we closed our eyes and bowed our heads, the Spirit descended on us all. Her prayer was eloquent and beautiful. She thanked the Lord for the Book of Mormon and for the teachings of the Church. She prayed for us, for our branch, and especially for her husband and son. I've never felt the Spirit so strongly in my entire life. At that moment, I understood the verse "the Spirit of God like a fire is burning." As we walked home afterward, the cold weather and the many cold rejections we experienced this week seemed insignificant. We were warmed.

Sad Outcome

We were sent the second missionary to be called from a former Soviet republic that is now a separate country. During the four months he was with us, I was impressed with his earnestness, humility, and good intentions. But his old drug habit soon took over—on repeated occasions. The substance—airplane glue—is easily purchased on a missionary's allowance and is obtainable at any stationery store.

After arriving at the mission-office entrance to be confronted about still another occurrence, he bolted and went AWOL. Only two weeks later, we learned that he was in jail in the distant city of Novgorod. We notified his family, and his LDS brother accompanied us there to take him back to his home on medical leave. The president of the elder's home mission was prepared to assist him in a rehabilitation program, an offer that the elder refused. [A year later, I was informed he died when he drove off a freeway in his home country.]

Windfall

Famed Candy Bomber of the Berlin airlift era, Gail Halvorsen, and his wife, Alta, have joined us as our latest seminary and institute supervisors. I've also called Elder Halvorsen to supervise missionwide Sunday School teacher training, logistics for BYU performing groups, and the mission's newly formed Young Men's committee. His limited Russian has been no obstacle. At seventy-five, Gail outdoes every young man in the mission—heading the pack on overnight excursions, following through on every assignment, and not allowing anyone else to fail either. Always there with his broad smile and warm handshake, he's made me look *really* good.

Courtesy Morgan Magleby

The "Candy Bomber." Elder Morgan Magleby poses with Elder Gail Halvorsen, the renowned Candy Bomber of the Berlin Airlift. Elder Halvorsen served as a mission seminary and institute supervisor.

Worship of Men

A member's antagonistic father and the father's friends came to me a while back, petitioning me to prevail on the member not to take legal action against the father. Under the circumstances, the lawsuit was none of my or the Church's business. I was thus fairly brusque, urging the father to become reconciled with his son, who happens to be one of our district presidents. Though the mood was strained, verging on hostile, a woman in their party literally knelt before me as the group departed. She was conditioned, I suppose, to genuflect before religious authority. But I was aghast. What groveling obsequiousness—in this case lacking any real underlying respect or understanding.

Then, just days ago, a representative of the mayor's office asked to see me on a matter related to our "Holy Father's" (i.e., Elder Boyd K. Packer's) forthcoming trip to St. Petersburg. I wanted to shout, "No. We don't consider our General Authorities 'Fathers!' We're all 'Brethren'— 'Brethren and Sisters.' There's only one Holy Father, and you've yet to learn who he is!"

Surveillance

We—and I assume all other "sects"—are being more closely watched right now than ever before. After our return flight from Kaliningrad last week, we were met in the plane before disembarking by a kindly, middle-aged gentleman who knowingly addressed us as "Mormons." He asked if our documents were in order and then welcomed us to St. Petersburg.

Later that day, as I talked to a reporter from the *St. Petersburg Press*, he asked me if our phone was bugged—implying that he'd picked up the signal of a listening device. We also know that the local security police manage to acquire copies of our in-house missionary phone and address list. They've even shown it to us. But being as open as we are—and as law-abiding—I believe we do not have any serious reason to fear.

Lumped

We seem to be getting more opposition right now, though not on an official level. Maybe it's a foreshadowing of the upcoming elections, compounded by political dissatisfaction with Yeltsin and aggravation over the events in Chechnya. But we are also too often lumped in the public mind with other groups—particularly the Moonies, Jehovah's Witnesses, Hari Krishnas, and Scientologists—which have generally left a bad impression. It doesn't help that some of these groups tend to coerce their adherents and even extort from them.

Another source of opposition is the so-called Christian Research Center, which is backed by American fundamentalists. It has united four other Protestant groups against us in Vyborg and is now doubly alarmed that we are building a chapel there.

His Church

I don't like to hear members talk about "*our* church." I wish they would get rid of that expression, because we don't own it. It's *His* church.

Undiluted

From Elder Benjamin Horton:

> Three of our investigators have committed to baptism—a mother, daughter, and son. The greatest thing about it is that they have committed their hearts.

> They live on the last stairway of a large complex. For six months, I had tracted their huge building with two different companions. It was worth it. We invited them to be baptized after the second discussion, but they would commit only to pray. We kept visiting them and took them to church and to others' baptisms, but their prompting to be baptized did not come until this week.

Elder Dustin Condren and I entered their apartment in the usual manner, but this time they seemed especially eager to begin the discussion. I asked them, as I had before, whether or not they had received their "answer." They smiled and said, "Yes. We want to be baptized."

Others have committed to baptism before, but this family's response really struck me. I knew their answer was not a conditioned response. I knew they were not attaching themselves to a pleasant social milieu and were not after American money. This family committed themselves because God had told them it was true. I did not convert them. Our Heavenly Father did. This helped me to understand that a true and pure testimony is possible. I hope I can gain a testimony as genuine as theirs.

Extending Her Borders

The Church will shortly be sending missionaries for the first time to Kazan, the Tartar-populated city on the North Volga. A museum worker there, who is also a scholar of comparative religions, became convinced that the LDS faith must be the true one since it is so heavily maligned by just about everyone else. Spurred by this logic, he traveled overnight with his wife to Samara to find the missionaries. After successive trips there, during which they continued to be taught the gospel, they were both baptized.

Quick Departures

Elaine Pagels contends that early Christianity became extremely diverse at a very early point in time, which only substantiates what we have all along understood about the Great Apostasy. As I monitor our nearly thirty units (branches and groups), I've learned that apostasy does not require a century or a year or a month but can happen within a single week.

For the first time, we are encountering former leaders who draw away other members and disparage the existing Church. Invariably, the dissent started when members began to bypass the established priesthood line of authority in arriving at decisions affecting the entire group. The safe countermode is—as we've been advised—to always govern by councils.

Young Men's service project. Service to others, such as remodeling a member's apartment, helped young Russian members transcend their immediate self-interest and learn the fundamentals of Christian living.

Eternal Vigilance

Branches of the Church seem, like plants, to have their individual cycle of promising fresh growth, then stagnation, even decay. The mission's "hot spots" keep shifting, and the strongest missionary support gets shifted accordingly. So much stems from the dedication, or lack of it, of the man in charge—the branch president. If the branch itself does not have a spirit of closeness and unity, then when people, including investigators, come to it, it will not be the draw it should be for them.

We also have the worrisome phenomenon of stagnation of the older "generations"—people who once were active, who once held positions but after being released failed to understand that we all serve only for a period of time. They are offended when they can no longer be in charge. Indeed, we need in most instances to issue new calls along with releases and during the interview emphasize that an eventual release is built into every call.

Strange Bedfellows

A mission makes for strange bedfellows. I was summoned twice to the dreaded headquarters of the Russian Federal Security Service, whose predecessors are the KGB. There I had to give a deposition about an LDS American who had run afoul of their law. I simply told the authorities what little I know of him, as a number of local members were also required to do. But since then, the Security Service has asked me to translate a letter addressed to a U.S. federal agency. I was more than happy to oblige, but I suppose that means I've been working for the former KGB.

Profound Lesson

From Elder Ken Packer:

> Last night I learned what the Atonement really means. My two companions and I had arranged several appointments at the same hour. Each of us was going to take as a companion one of three young boys who had recently joined the Church. But it all fell apart. One boy had forgotten, and the other had fallen ill. We still had two companionships but work for three. We then decided to delay the appointment with Nikolay until later that evening.
>
> When we finally reached Nikolay's door, we were met by a member of the Church, who gave us a scolding. She said that we didn't know what we were doing and that Nikolay would never be baptized because he was so offended he had just spent the last two hours yelling

at his wife. I prayed with all my heart that the Lord would make things right in view of his servants' poor judgment.

As we entered the room, the Spirit softened all of our hearts. That moment was the turning point for Nikolay. We could see it, and he could feel it. The Lord does make up the difference.

[Nikolay was baptized and later served as the branch president in Tosno.]

Grave Oversight

As we constantly admonish one another to keep the commandments, we too often fail to remember which two commandments are "the greatest" (Matt. 22:36–40).

Glue

If there were ever a Mormon Florence Nightingale, I'd nominate Sister Irina Bereznyak. She is always there behind the scenes, doing the cleanup after meetings. She nurses other members' dying parents, attends each of the four districts' conferences, and eagerly promotes cooperative work ventures with other members.

A chemist by profession, she was the first in her enterprise to renounce her Party affiliation when such an action was still precarious. Like so many others, she was deserted by her husband and contends with her only child, a fairly unmanageable and unappreciative teenage daughter. Russian women are, by contrast with many of the men, so strong, accountable, and hard working— truly the glue that holds this nation together.

A Mormon Florence Nightingale. Sister Irina Bereznyak spends much of her time caring for others without public recognition.

A Natural

I was first struck by his surname, Lermontov, which he shares with one of Russia's foremost poets. Then, after casting him as the lead in both of our mission plays, I came to recognize his remarkable charismatic gift—whether on stage or off, it was the same. He had so much integrity and such a simple solid faith. A student of electrical engineering, he had no noticeable aesthetic inclinations or prior experience. But radiating so much of his own true self, he was meant to be the lead in our mission-produced plays. I seriously doubt we could have performed them without him.

What unity and esprit those plays conjured, especially within each cast. So many cast members have since served full-time missions, and some of the nonmembers of the casts have since been baptized. Activities of this order are what the Church needs more of. And I still contend that *everyone* can be an actor.

Strange Logic

An interesting case was recently reported to me by a branch president. An inactive member who was an alcoholic before her baptism had another of her rare lapses. During that bout of drinking, she physically attacked an older woman, who is now bringing her to trial. The inactive member complains that the Church is remiss in not keeping life and religion in separate spheres, as does the Orthodox tradition.

Where would she be today, I asked, if the Church did not consider all physical things to be equally spiritual? Wouldn't she still be a thoroughgoing alcoholic?

Good Luck!

A former mission youth leader—big hearted but still rather young and not always so wise—was in trouble with the Mafia as an indebted vegetable hawker. Members assisted him in settling elsewhere incognito, hopefully undetected.

Tapestry

Besides mostly Americans, our missionary force has been a rich blend—two Australians, one Brit, two East Germans, two Swedes, one Finn, a sister from Moldavia, one Czech, one Hungarian, a half-dozen Ukarainians, several native Russians, and, surely the most exotic thread of all, a Peruvian who had studied agronomy for several years in Rostov before his mission call. Among those from the States are a Black and a half-Chinese. Among the members here are several from Africa and others of Jewish, Caucasian, or partial Tartar descent. This mission has produced a remarkable blending of brothers and sisters whose diverse nationalities and racial origin recede in importance before all that is precious that we have in common. Our blend further attests to the global kinship of all God's children—both spiritual and at times quite literal.

Diversity in the ranks. Elder Oleg Goncharenko is a mellow Ukrainian who, with three other Ukrainian elders and three Ukrainian sisters, served a mission in St. Petersburg.

Wistful Close: Spring 1996

Another Strange Bedfellow

We've had visits from a catacomb (unofficial) priest, "Father Aleksey." I deliberately slip and call him "Brother." He holds liturgical services twice weekly on the city's outskirts in his ninth-floor apartment, usually with a retinue of three other faithful disciples—two of them female, the third an apprentice monk. When, at Aleksey's insistence, I attended one such service, I took my first counselor. The service lasted for two straight hours. Fortunately, they made an exception for me and provided a chair. The rest stood.

I'd always been transported by the reverent, soulful mood of the Orthodox services I'd attended in times past—usually only a brief segment accompanied by an ethereal a cappella choir. But Aleksey's interminable repetition of the names of Deity and saints, the incense he frequently wafted in our faces, the elaborate communion—all performed (and consumed) by Father Aleksey—struck me for the first time as both meaningless and oppressive.

Aleksey is as uncomfortable with our services. To my amazement, he has asked us to baptize him, while making it perfectly clear that our comparatively sizable congregations badly need his ritual.

Enduring Care

From Elder Michael McDonald:

> Something I had never expected happened last night to our "perfect investigator." On Friday our zone leader, Elder Eric Blaser, did not pass Sasha during his baptismal interview. When Elder Jonathan Hart and I met again with Sasha, we discovered a concern that had been rather well hidden. Sasha has been reading some anti-Mormon literature. In short, we found that Sasha is nowhere near ready for baptism.
>
> Although Elder Hart and I spent about three hours pleading with Sasha to pray about the truthfulness of the Book of Mormon, we went home feeling very empty. This morning at church, I couldn't help but think of how Sasha is missing the opportunity to partake of the sacrament and turn his thoughts upon the Savior. It doesn't seem fair

that things would end up this way. I will always remember Sasha and pray the opportunity presents itself to him another time.

Perplexing

We have been visited socially from time to time by a charming member couple I met here by chance before we came to preside in the mission. At the time of our first encounter in 1991, they were eagerly translating materials from the *Ensign* for the fledgling Russian mission, and their precocious young son enthusiastically expounded the gospel to the entire local priesthood. In consequence, we helped sponsor him as one of the first Russian students to attend BYU. I'd also understood that his father had meanwhile been called as a branch president. But by the time we arrived on the scene two years later, something had changed. The son was still at BYU but, like his parents, was fairly inactive and far from enthusiastic about the Church.

With each of their visits to the office, the parents have announced some kind of personal need and sought some sort of favor. Within reason, I've always tried to assist. But there's never been much reciprocation, particularly in terms of enthusiastic or accountable Church service—unless they believe they will gain some material advantage. Their requests are so blatant, the inequity so obvious, that I am embarrassed even to hint at it to them, though I'm always dumbfounded.

Merriam and I like the family, and I think they like us. But never have I encountered anyone so unabashedly intent on taking without the least desire to give in return. This is especially unexpected on the part of those who were once quite otherwise.

Esprit

The number of full-time native missionaries serving from St. Petersburg was two when we arrived and is now thirteen. There may be as many as twenty by year's end. These missionaries come from a close-knit group of older teenage youth that was formed during our second summer when they attended a missionary training class and thereafter served as district missionaries. Simultaneously, a number of them made up the cast of our first mission play production—a Russian adaptation of *The Brothers Karamazov*. At other times, they also participated prominently in semiannual youth conferences. Now, as each departs by train or plane for his or her mission field, those not yet called invariably come to cheer and see their friend off.

Super Saturday. Kolya Patrushev, later a full-time missionary who served in Ukraine, leads the youth in a "getting to know you" game.

Brother Pavel

We had such endearing visits the many times he came to see me—both before he was baptized and after. He was a such a kind, gentle person. But from the very start he had an ulterior purpose and would never let it go. He'd already read the Book of Mormon when we first met, and he testified it was scripture. Then he produced his own supplementary verses to the Gospel of John, showing me how they harmonized with the restored gospel. I asked where he'd gotten them. He hedged but insisted we call them to the attention of the prophet. (It was President Hunter then.) I obliged by passing them on to our Area Presidency. I already knew what they would say.

He took it gracefully but not lying down. He next traveled to Utah and procured an audience with several members of the Seventy. He attended the Russian ward in Salt Lake City, where he qualified for baptism. I learned of this before he returned to St. Petersburg. He even gave me a copy of the book he'd picked up in California, Benjamin T. Cullen's *The Book of Jesus*, to prove there are other channels of revelation. But he still has never really involved himself with the members. I'm sorry. He and I are still at an impasse. And he's such a nice man!

Worrisome

He's a high-placed Church leader, and we get along well enough. But he's always so effusive, so verbal, so sure of himself—into political causes or commercial ventures and solicitations for funding from the Church or its stateside members. He protests too often that he's no Ostap Bender—the Soviet's infamous literary "wheeler-dealer" *(veliky kombinator)*. And, I fear, he doesn't really listen well—either to me or to the many members who need to be heard before he expresses care and offers counsel. He also takes abrupt, periodic "vacations" from his Church service. I worry that he might not hold out, particularly after his eventual release.

Hidden Agendas

In the eyes of so many who come to me with their own hidden agendas, I am very important, not because they respect what I have to tell them, but because they think they can get something out of me. I'll provide my successor with a long, confidential list of con artists, predators, charlatans, end runners, and pests—both members and nonmembers—before I leave. They will doubtless want to "have at him" too, and it will help him to be forewarned.

Lacuna

Our young members need basic training in the fundamentals of courtship. Case in point: A very earnest and committed convert, age twenty-seven, was induced last fall—about the time of his baptism—to propose to a young woman with an illegitimate child. They had been acquainted only a week. She apparently made a play for him to obtain better housing, and he's had utter hell to pay ever since. The new wife is a shoplifter who abuses them all (including her three-year-old daughter by a former lover). She stays away all night, sleeping around with one or another "uncle," as the child calls each of them.

The saintly, well-meaning husband still wants to reform her. Meanwhile, she continues to mock him and his mother for their piety and resents the slightest correction. She recently lost a fetus, probably deliberately, and would like her husband and his mother to give up their current three-room apartment for two separate apartments with two rooms each. The two fear she will then tell her husband he can join his mother in one of the apartments and leave her with the other, knowing he would yield it to her and the child out of kindness.

144

Faulty Sample

An American brother who has worked here with certain members has sadly concluded the following:

> One thing I have learned in dealing with the Russian people is that the concept of freedom and letting people make their own decisions without being compelled to do so is still a foreign concept for our Russian brothers and sisters. I found that once they are given a position to serve in the Church they take it as some kind of social position. If they are asked to change that position or give it up so that someone else can have an opportunity to serve, they become offended. I think that it is just a matter of time as the spirit of Christ becomes part of their being and they understand the true meaning of what it means to be a brother and sister in the Church.

This analysis fails to account for a number of instances that illustrate the exact opposite. The manifestation of the spirit of Christ on the part of certain relatively new Russian members would put most homegrown Mormons in America to utter shame. With all that is so unpredictable in some members, there is also a steadiness in others that astounds and utterly inspires. They truly love the Lord and are ever there to serve him. Without such, where would we be? But with such, what can't we eventually accomplish?

Whom the Lord Loveth

From Elder Steven Scrogham:

> In August 1995, a group of anti-American thugs broke into a Sunday sacrament meeting in Kupchino. Nine months later, in May 1996, Elder Casey O'Dwyer and I moved apprehensively into our Kupchino apartment. We prayed that the Lord would bless us with courage and the Spirit to walk the streets in search of those He had prepared. Several weeks passed with no success, but we continued to work, knowing that at any time someone could respond to Christ's message.
>
> After another morning of street contacting characterized by rejection after rejection, we returned home. An unkempt man, leaning awkwardly against the doorway, greeted us as we entered our building. He appeared to be about forty years old. His clothes were filthy, his hair greasy, and he reeked of alcohol. We agreed to stop by his apartment the next day to share our message, but quite honestly, we saw Vitaly more as a way to get out of contacting than as a potential investigator.
>
> The next day at 2:00 P.M. we knocked on the door of Vitaly's second floor apartment. It was clear he had been drinking. He was unable

to comprehend the purpose of our meeting and seemed interested only in talking about America. Vitaly obviously had a severe problem with alcohol that he would need to overcome if he were to progress with the discussions. Nonetheless, we left a Book of Mormon on the coat rack in the hall, and he agreed to be sober the next time we came.

The next visit was no better than the first. Vitaly was still not in a state to even begin discussing gospel principles. After several more short, unproductive visits, we dropped him from our list of serious investigators. This wasn't the end of our contact with Vitaly, however. Days later we saw him walking on the opposite side of Kupchinskaya Street. His clothes were clean and his hair combed. But given the quality of our prior visits, we didn't even consider inviting him to hear more about the gospel.

As summer got under way, my new companion, Elder Brian Sorensen, and I were walking through a courtyard when we saw in front of us a confident, well-dressed man. As he came nearer, I again recognized Vitaly. I couldn't believe this was the man who only weeks earlier had tried to talk me into helping him get to America. As we talked, Vitaly told us of his changed lifestyle. He had quit drinking, regularly pondered the gospel of Jesus Christ, and often discussed the Book of Mormon with several of his friends.

Our subsequent visits in Vitaly's living room were overwhelmingly filled with the Holy Spirit. He was so excited about the plan of salvation. Despite the happiness I felt while watching this man learn and accept the gospel, I had yet to hear the most amazing thing about his conversion. Vitaly had been among those who because of their protests were forced to the floor by the thugs during the August 1995 sacrament meeting. Even before his baptism, this man had openly defended The Church of Jesus Christ of Latter-day Saints in the face of persecution.

For nearly a year, something within Vitaly—maybe the stand he took on that occasion—caused him to remain sensitive to the truth of the gospel, even as he struggled to live one of its important principles.

[Vitaly was baptized in December 1996, then involved in missionary work and given the priesthood.]

Local Encounters

Elder Jake Keller recently engaged an Orthodox priest who said he was aware of our missionaries but had gone out of his way not to speak to them. As he put it, the Orthodox priests fear us. They don't know the scriptures as well as we, he maintained, relying more on theological commentaries.

They also envy the way we manage to engage their people by testifying to them. Most of their worshipers only come to them, he admitted, because of tradition. "What is more important to conform to, tradition or the true gospel of Jesus Christ?" Elder Keller then asked. The answer: tradition, because that is what the people want.

Marina Lutikova, one of our Russian sister missionaries from Moscow, described another very personal encounter with Orthodoxy:

> My companion and I attended an Orthodox service last week. For me it was the first time, and I found it very interesting. During the service I prayed to know if what was taking place pleased God. I did not feel the Spirit, only emptiness. I saw many people, standing in darkness. I did not see light in their eyes, and I felt oppressed. On Sunday, as I attended our services, though the meeting hall was chilly, my spirit was warm and I saw light in people's eyes, smiles, happiness, and joy. The prayers were personal and full of feeling. Once more I was persuaded that I had made the right choice when I joined the Church.

Conversion of a Priest

From Elder Joel Beus:

> Although Aleksandr Bulgakov had a good job as a journalist in the early 1980s, when he was young, he decided he needed to find God. He decided to enter a monastery in spite of his family's warning that they would disown him if he became a monk. He hasn't had any contact with his family since.
>
> While in the monastery, he learned Hebrew and became a gifted Bible scholar, but his greatest desire was to have the Holy Ghost in his life. After four years, he determined that the Holy Ghost was not to be found in the monastery. He discussed his discovery with other monks and informed them he was thinking of leaving the monastery for that reason. They derided him and said that he'd never find the Holy Ghost anywhere because no one is worthy of that gift in our time. He left anyway, and for many years, he visited all the churches he could find. Nowhere could he find the Holy Ghost.
>
> In summer 1996, he was considering reentering a monastery in Moscow. During a phone call, he agreed to join a friend at a church service in Moscow. Just as he hung up, my companion walked up to the pay phone and started talking to him.
>
> Because he was always glad to talk about religion, he agreed to meet with us. We taught him a first discussion but soon discovered he had already concluded that modern-day prophets, priesthood authority, and continued revelation are needed. We instructed him to read

147

and pray about the Book of Mormon and Joseph Smith, and we discussed the Holy Ghost.

After we left that night, he read the passages in the copy of the Book of Mormon we had given him and then went out on his balcony and prayed. Later he told us that he'd had an incredible spiritual manifestation that convinced him not only of the truthfulness of the Book of Mormon but also of the reality of the Holy Ghost. The next Sunday he joined us in church and bore his testimony of the truthfulness of the gospel. He said he had been somewhat shocked by Moroni 10:3–5 and by our straightforward invitation to ask God whether the message is true. We were the boldest missionaries he'd ever met from any church, he added, because we had acted as if the Holy Ghost was in the next room wanting to come and visit him. Then during his prayer, he had realized just how close the Holy Ghost was and how willing the Spirit was to visit him.

During the rest of the discussions, it was amazing how many of the principles and conclusions we presented he had already accepted as true. In fact, he taught us much more than we taught him. He read the entire Book of Mormon in less then two weeks, and before his baptism, he recorded the entire text on tape so that he could listen to it as he painted (he sells paintings for a living). Soon after, he became a district missionary, no doubt one of the most knowledgeable district missionaries in the history of the Church.

The Brethren

Again, after rubbing shoulders at close quarters with another Apostle, my impression is that up close they are relatively casual, very much themselves, positively encouraging, and nondictatorial. We were similarly inspired by our Area Presidency's counsel to various mission presidents and priesthood leaders:

> Our most important task is to act as the Lord would act, be sufficiently (not overly) confident, and be submissive. (Elder Dennis B. Neuenschwander)

> The missionaries take their callings too lightly. No one understands better than do the Brethren that [the rules the missionaries follow] are not from them. (Elder Dennis B. Neuenschwander)

> Leadership is finding the divine potential in each member of our group, stimulating creative energy, and having the vision and faith in what has not yet been achieved. (Elder Charles Didier)

> The Church is not run by experience alone or the wisdom derived from experience but by revelation. (Elder Bruce D. Porter)

Tough Call

A number of outstanding young members of missionary age are unable to serve because they are unwilling to register for armed service. Who can blame them? The abuse of new recruits and the heavy loss of Russian lives in the country's questionable venture in Chechnya would incite cynicism and fear in anyone. Still, the Church cannot afford to send these young men to other places and thus unwittingly assist them to avoid their obligation as citizens.

There are notable exceptions like Roman Batin, the son of an earlier branch president who had one day simply walked away from his calling and never returned to our meetings. Roman has all along remained enthusiastically involved, as has his younger brother. When it was time for Roman to register for the draft, he did not hesitate in doing so. Despite his youth, he was then a counselor in the East District presidency. He has since been stationed near enough to St. Petersburg that on weekends he often manages to attend meetings in his home branch. I imagine that, at some point, a full-time mission will follow.

Sowing

From Elder Dustin Condren:

> This week Elder Daniel Robrecht and I have been contacting by the *rynok* [outdoor market] here in Vyborg. We hadn't found too many interested people until the day we were approached by a middle-aged man. He asked us if he could have a copy of the Doctrine and Covenants. That was an unusual request from a stranger, and I immediately suspected he was from the local Christian Center, which agitates against the Church. So I became defensive. I told him that, because the Doctrine and Covenants had just been released, there weren't enough copies for all who wanted them.
>
> Then this man pulled an old copy of the Book of Mormon from out of his bag and told us he'd received it from another missionary a couple of years before and that he'd read it and knew it was true. We then told him that we wanted to meet with him. We took him to the chapel and taught him the first and second discussions. There he told us he'd had a dream after reading the Book of Mormon. In the dream, he saw a light and was told that there is only one true church.
>
> This man had also shared the Book of Mormon with his mother. She had read it and told him that any sane person would join the church that was the source of that book. In addition, he'd shown the book to several other people with whom he met to read it on a regular basis.

Elder Robrecht and I were overwhelmed by what we'd stumbled onto. We invited the man to be baptized, and he accepted our invitation. Unfortunately, he had to return to Pskov immediately and, since we have no missionaries there, he still couldn't be fully involved in the Church. So we gave him several copies of the Book of Mormon, the Doctrine and Covenants he'd asked for, and several copies of the *Liahona*.

We could only hope the Lord would look out for him and his friends until other missionaries would come to Pskov.

[Pskov has since been opened, as have a number of other cities—including Petrozavodsk and Novgorod—where a number of lone members and investigators were already in place.]

Hearts of the Children

For the second time, we've heard Maksim Shostakovich conduct a symphony by his father, Dmitry, in the philharmonic hall named for the father. On the first occasion, as the audience vociferously applauded him, Maksim inserted a carnation in his father's score and held it up to our view as if to say, "It's his work you're applauding, not me." This time he again held up the score and then kissed it. The very essence of our message: "The hearts of the children turning to their fathers." If only all sons and daughters felt that way.

What Meets the Eye

Concerted opposition, stage managed by the Christian Research Institute, has continually confronted the Church in Vyborg. This is surely why it took us four years to get the city fathers' permission for a building site and further authorizations. Now that the building has been completed and dedicated, local citizens come to that beautiful edifice voluntarily asking for baptism, which never happened before. Buildings make a difference!

Perspective

From Elder David Flanagan:

In the city of Setraretsk, the Mafia are not quite as evident as in more urban Petersburg. But one morning, Elder William Stevens and I noticed a heavy-set Mafia type sitting on the bench outside our stairwell. We hurried past him to grab some more literature from our apartment. Not fifteen minutes later, we exited onto a scene of sheer pandemonium.

Police were everywhere, and the man we'd noticed earlier now lay life-less, under a bloody sheet. This was my most intimate brush with death, and its violence disturbed me deeply.

Early the next morning, I watched one of our local priesthood holders baptize our friend and investigator, Lena, in the crystal waters of Sestraretsk Lake. The city still slept, and a cool summer drizzle reflected the early morning sun. Within eighteen hours, I had seen a frighteningly violent display of death and a profoundly beautiful spiritual birth. God gave me perspective on that quiet lake shore.

Image

One of our members cannot recognize or accept the concerned solicitations of our most devoted priesthood leaders. She acts much like a she-wolf backed to the wall who with defiant snarls and bared teeth defends her young against the threatening intruder. In blessing her disheartened leaders, I reminded them that they must never reject her. Each of those good men immediately received a witness that that was the correct and only possible answer.

Courtesy Jon Reynolds

Vyborg chapel. Despite much opposition from both government and religious authorities, the Vyborg chapel, the first LDS chapel constructed in Russia, was finally dedicated May 4, 1996.

Celestial Weddings

The precedent of two "celestial weddings" will do much to inspire the members and send familial roots deep into the Russian soil. The student Oleg Martaler is Vyborg's quiet, committed seminary teacher and now a counselor in the Vyborg district presidency. He and his bride from the same community will be the first of our members to marry in the Stockholm temple. (The temple wedding will, of course, follow the obligatory registration ceremony at a local Russian wedding office—but by only a few days).

The second such union is, I believe, also unique to the Church in Russia. It involves two former full-time missionaries: the vivacious Natasha Smirnova, whom I set apart two years ago and who served in the Ukraine Kiev Mission, and the fine Igor Akolyushny,

Russian pioneer. Oleg Martaler coordinated the seminary and institute programs in Vyborg. He and his wife were the first Russian couple to be married in the Stockholm Sweden Temple.

who hails from Ukraine but faithfully served his mission in St. Petersburg. Igor returned here a year after his release, unable to find work in his destitute country. He also has the distinction of having joined the Church after the first American missionaries came to East Germany, where he was serving as a member of the occupying Red Army. This deed alone says volumes about his courage and independence, not to mention his great faith. Not long ago, he came to me, wondering if despite his being almost thirty he should defer marriage for further education. I take credit for saying, "No," and tilting his resolve by pointing him in Natasha's direction.

Wistfully

Bakaev, Batin, Batyanov, Grigorev, Mariev, Natanadze, Pozdeev, Savchenko, Shalamov, Shupovalov, Tuaev. For me, these eleven names have a special,

Igor and Natasha Akolyushny. Both served full-time missions—she in Ukraine, he as a Ukrainian Russian in St. Petersburg. They were the first Russian returned missionaries to be married in the Stockholm temple. Igor may also be the only Russian who joined the Church while still a member of the Soviet army occupying East Germany.

sad ring to them. I associate each with a man I have personally known and admired. Each has in his time inspired me. Each was once a branch president. None are now active. "Sticking power"—that's something we must try to help our members learn.

Dear friends, the Church is not a two- or three-year course in general education that then certifies you to move on. The covenants you made at baptism were not contracted with the missionaries or with the Church but with your Savior. They're lifelong—and then some. Chances are you will never read this, but, should you do so, I won't apologize. I hope it nudges you some. Then it will be worth it.

Unforeseen Blessing

In at least one respect, Merriam's and my mission has been particularly fruitful. The unprecedented addition of seven more grandchildren since we came away brings the present total to eighteen. Though we have surely missed each of our family members during this three-year absence, we were assured by Elder Oaks's blessing. As he set us apart, he told us we need not be concerned for our children's welfare, for they would adequately manage their affairs without us. That has certainly been the case. We would urge other senior couples who might serve missions but have such concerns to place their trust in the Lord's care and keeping. By doing so, we and our family were blessed in profound, unaccountable ways.

Deeply Rooted

On the eve of our departure, General Aleksandr Lebed made a crude slur against Mormons—"mold and slime"—during the electoral campaign. Although it sounds quite ominous, we hope it's merely an idle threat. However, even if the Church has to go underground, it will survive here with the strong, devoted members and leaders we now have in place. I couldn't have said that earlier, but now I can.

Personal Note

On the same day that President Gary Anderson arrives and we are officially released—July 2, 1996—Will, our youngest son, will marry Natasha Vladimirovna Belikova in a local ZAGS (State wedding "palace"). They met here two years ago in his classroom when he first began to teach English. We trust he will always remember how much he owes to our call to the Russia St. Petersburg Mission. And on that note, this account of another LDS mission ends.

Final Thoughts

Rimma

Karen Hall

With Sister Karen Hall's permission, I append her account of a particularly wrenching experience with an investigator. It evokes the missionaries' frequent close attachment to those they teach and the occasional shock, even numbness, when such persons, including recent new members, fail to follow through as expected. It also suggests the stoic courage missionaries must call upon in order to weather bitter disappointment and to not despair. Encounters like this, as well as daily rejection from most of those they contact, bespeak the faithful, persistent missionary's remarkable heroism.

The first time I met Rimma, we taught her about the plan of salvation and eternal life and committed her to live the law of chastity and the Word of Wisdom. The discussion was at the house of a member who was Rimma's friend from work. Rimma seemed like a very nice woman with a wry sense of humor. We unconsciously and naively congratulated ourselves on the success of the discussion. Only one week in Kolpino and already we had a candidate for baptism.

After the initial meeting, however, we discovered that it would be more difficult than we expected to get Rimma to stop smoking. We decided to set up more frequent meetings with her at her apartment, while continuing to meet periodically with her member friend.

I don't remember the lesson we gave Rimma the first night at her apartment, but I remember my impressions of her home. It was a very small one-room apartment—one of the smallest I'd seen. But I'd been in Russia long enough to completely disregard housing problems. Her bed, Anochka's crib (Anya was her three-year-old daughter), a large wardrobe, a small table, and a shelf plastered with beer and vodka ads holding a small TV were the only furnishings in the small room.

Anya was a very boisterous child who spoke a lot but with a childish lisp. She couldn't hold still for very long and loved to have us come visit. Her mother later told us that the threat she used to make Anya behave was that the sisters wouldn't come over anymore. Even that couldn't calm her down. I remember sitting in Rimma's apartment more than once when suddenly Anya would climb on the shelf, grab me by the neck, and hang there, yelling, "I can strangle you, all the way strangle you. *Vot!*"

Anya's violence was matched only by that of the cat, whose eyes literally glowed red-orange in the right light. She could be lying on the carpet one minute, then jump up and dash around the room at breakneck speed until Anya grabbed her by the tail. The cat soon discovered under my skirt the thermal underwear that became exposed when I took my long boots off to enter Rimma's apartment. It was not unusual to feel the cat crawling up my leg and onto my lap, under my skirt. The cat's trick, Rimma showed us to our dismay, was to drink your spit if you drooled on your chin.

Despite the lively surroundings, we had some wonderful gospel discussions with Rimma. She had insights into the Book of Mormon that I didn't expect. We quickly grew to love her; she returned that love and was always thrilled to see us. She began making real progress in giving up smoking. October and November flew by, and we set a baptismal date for Christmas Eve.

Winter didn't slow down missionary work in Kolpino, but it slowed me down. Unused to the humidity, extreme cold, darkness, and pollution, I came down with a case of bronchitis that wouldn't go away and eventually turned into walking pneumonia. I also had had some problems with my companion and got a different companion during transfers. I was feeling guilt from that episode. I felt only pressure, and not support, from the other missionaries in my area and found myself struggling to feel the Spirit and keep going. I was afraid I would be sent home, but I was also afraid that I couldn't survive the winter. Among my few solaces were the relationships we had with our investigators.

As time went by, we started to learn more about Rimma's past life. She was an orphan, raised in a children's home. She had given birth to a little boy who would be eleven now, but he was dead. Her husband, Anya's father, died a year prior to our meeting her. Previous to his death, they had both been alcoholics, but after he died, Rimma stopped drinking. I looked at Anya and realized that her little face wasn't quite perfect. Her forehead was very high, and her eyes were set wide apart. These features, combined with her hyperactivity, made me realize that she was probably a fetal alcohol syndrome baby.

Rimma's economic situation was also depressing. She worked as a seamstress for a firm that didn't regularly pay its employees. Sometimes she had nothing to feed Anya, so the old man and woman downstairs would feed her while Rimma went hungry. We ached for her hardships but kept assuring her that only through the gospel could she find pure solace. She held onto that faith, and we held onto her. She was truly becoming our spiritual sister.

In mid-December Rimma, probably malnourished and exhausted from work, came down with a violent respiratory illness. She struggled to get well and in desperation began smoking again. Afraid of her illness, we stopped by Rimma's only a couple of times before New Year's.

Courtesy Karen Hall

Karen Hall

Two days after New Year's, we went to Rimma's apartment. She was drunk. She explained that her old drinking buddies had stopped by during the holidays and persuaded her to have a "caplet" of champagne. The temptation was too much, and being an alcoholic, she couldn't stop. She was completely drunk and had been so for several days.

Rimma was ashamed to see us but invited us in. I'll remember that afternoon as the day I lost my innocent naiveté. Her normally tidy apartment was a mess and smelled like urine and beer. In her drunken and ashamed state, she confessed to us that she could never get baptized; she had committed a sin she couldn't be forgiven for. She said that her husband's death wasn't an accident. They had both been drunk and fighting. She shoved him, and he fell down the stairs and died. As a matter of fact, they weren't even really married; they had just been living together. She told us that her son wasn't dead, but she had put him in a children's home and lied about it to Anya. She admitted that once in a while, before she met us, she had prostituted herself to feed her child.

We realized why her baptism had been put off so many times. She had all this unresolved guilt and didn't think that the Atonement of Jesus Christ applied to her. We assured her that her husband's death was an accident, that the Atonement did apply to her, and that she could be healed only through Christ. She was very comforted by our words and promised to go to work the next day.

We stopped by early the next morning to make sure that she was up and that Anya was going to preschool and to give her some Advil. She was on her way out. We rejoiced that she was on the path back and stopped by her house that night. But she had lost her job and was drunk again.

This binge lasted about two weeks. We had almost given up on her when we stopped by and found her completely sober. She had found a new job as a janitor at a school. Not only would she be paid regularly, but they would also feed her lunch every day. We got her back on a reading schedule, set a new baptismal date, and began working with her again.

A week later, she started drinking once more. We stopped by Saturday afternoon. Her house was in shambles, Anya was running around naked, and Rimma was drinking brown liquid out of a large bottle with a huge fungus sponge on top (my first acquaintance with *grib*). She was once again repentant and promised to stop drinking. These drunk-sober-drunk episodes lasted until I was transferred. The horrible realizations increased every time she got drunk. One time we found her coming up the stairs with a strange man and her daughter. By her shocked look and explanations, we realized that she was resorting to prostitution to provide drinking money.

Every time Rimma was drunk, the old woman downstairs would say, "I told you and I'll tell you again, she is an unrighteous, incorrigible person. No one will ever change her." When Rimma was sober, the old woman would praise us, praise God, and ask if she could come to one of our revivals. We felt that we just couldn't let go. We loved her too much, and it was our calling to help people come to Christ, no matter who they were.

The situation came to a horrible climax in February. After a promising sober period, my new threesome companions and I went to Rimma's to teach a discussion. Anochka was in the house alone and said that, if she opened the door, her mother would beat her. Finally, scared and lonely, she opened the door and let us in. It was clear that Rimma had started to drink again. The old man downstairs came up and talked to us about the problem (he was more coherent than his wife). We cleaned up the apartment and played with Anya for a bit until Rimma came staggering home with a drunken friend. The old man lost all patience and began to shout at her so quickly that I couldn't keep up with the Russian. I understood, however, that he was accusing her of being a horrible mother. She screamed back, grabbed Anya, and ran for their fifth-story window. I suddenly understood that she meant to kill herself and Anya with her. One of my companions and I jumped in front of the window and pushed her back. She struggled for a while, then let go of Anya and sat down in the kitchen with her head in her hands.

For the next half hour, the old drunken friend tried to convince me that I should go buy Rimma some vodka; only vodka would make her feel better. "I'm not asking for myself. I'm only thinking of Rimma. See, she is suffering so much." Disgusted, I shook my head and gave them the best tongue lashing that I could manage in Russian. I just wanted to leave. I was very angry and very confused. Life wasn't supposed to be like this. Unfortunately, we didn't dare leave until Rimma calmed down. I didn't want the death of a three-year-old child on my conscience.

Some time passed, and Rimma told us she was going to the bathroom. Instead, she grabbed her coat, stole 20,000 rubles from my companion's pocket, and ran out the door, leaving us alone with Anya. We stayed with her until Rimma came home again late that night.

On the way home, I sat on the bus and felt on the verge of a nervous breakdown. I kept chanting to myself, "Trust in the Lord with all thine heart." The rhythm of the chant and the creaking bus lulled me somewhat. I had never felt so helpless and unsure of what to do. I felt certain that we would never be able to help her.

Soon after that episode, I received a transfer call. Sisters were leaving Kolpino altogether. I was hurt by the transfer, because I knew that my district leader had requested that we leave. I was also relieved in a very basic way. Rimma was now someone else's problem. I felt very guilty for having those feelings. Wasn't I supposed to love her unconditionally? I was horrified to discover that my love had limits. I was even more horrified to make this discovery on my mission.

That transfer was the low point of my mission and my life. The pressure of my own sickness, personality conflicts, and problems in proselytizing had hardened me. I no longer felt the Spirit or even the desire to read my scriptures. The transfer to a new branch in St. Petersburg was also one of the biggest blessings of my mission. I learned, for the first time in my life, what repentance was and struggled for a long time to gain back the joy that I had felt earlier on my mission. The joy did come back and the last five months of my mission were very fulfilling.

Soon it was time for me to go home. I learned that, after I left Kolpino, Rimma slipped through the cracks. The elders didn't go to her apartment because of the prostitution problem. There were no sisters in the town, and the members were too caught up in their own problems to get involved.

I was serving with a brand new sister and took her with me to visit some old investigators before I left for home. For each I had written my testimony on the back of a picture of the temple. One day we took a taxi and went down to Kolpino. I had told my companion all about Rimma and was anxious to see her again, but a little apprehensive about what I would find.

What I found was Rimma passed out on the doorstep of her apartment, wearing filthy clothes and smelling of alcohol. She didn't rouse when we approached her. I just stared for a minute, then my face hardened, and I put the picture of the temple, with my testimony about the love of Christ, in her pocket. We went downstairs and knocked on the old woman's door. She welcomed us and then explained that Rimma was finally evicted from her apartment because she couldn't pay the rent. The police had taken Anya away and put her in a children's home somewhere in St. Petersburg. Rimma had been drunk for a month. I silently ended the story in my head. In her condition, homeless and unhealthy, Rimma wouldn't survive the next winter. We left, after hearing the old woman's repeated "I told you so."

My companion was shocked that I greeted the news so nonchalantly. I wasn't shocked. I felt nothing—not pain, not sorrow, not sympathy. I reacted as if I had read about Rimma in some sociology textbook. Logically, I knew that Rimma was a human being like me. She had all the deep feelings and emotions I did. She was also a child of God like me, a recipient of his love like me. She was a profoundly unique individual like me. I knew I *should* feel sorrow. I didn't. I thought that maybe later I would cry. I haven't.

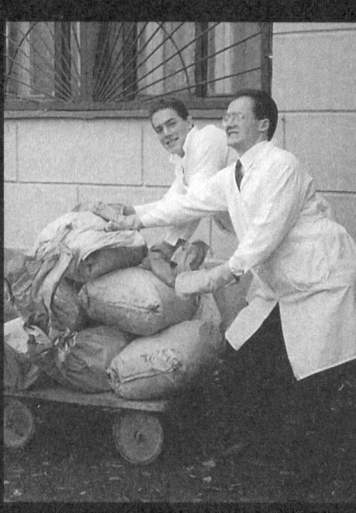

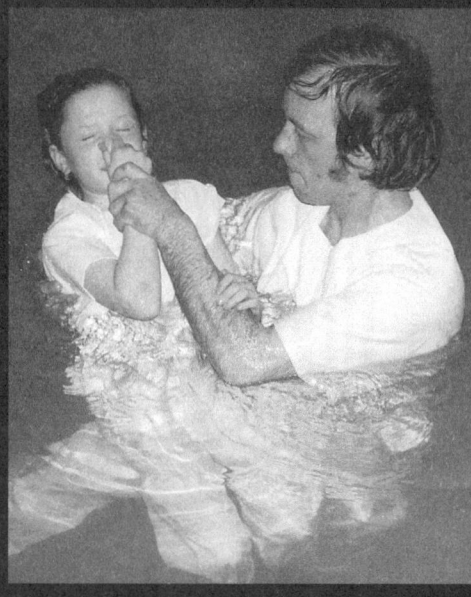

Looking Back

Affect

After we'd arrived in St. Petersburg and had sent back various journal entries, Don Jarvis wrote me, "You've certainly changed." It's good others can see how the gospel has seriously worked upon us—how it has indeed changed us—how we have repented. One of the Brethren has said that showing others how the gospel has caused us to repent is the most effective way to preach it. Or, as a great former assistant to the president, whom we still quote, put it, "The best missionary is a repenting missionary."

It is indeed a wonderful purgation and cleansing to be pulled out of our circle of worldly attachments and be exposed to the whole-souled goodness of so many who have consecrated themselves to the Lord's service. Consecration is the process required of every authentic convert and, in turn, of every missionary—mission presidents not excepted.

Team Spirit

I'd like to remember one thing: I never want to complicate the lives of my leaders in any way, beginning with my bishop. I don't want to tax him and ask for special dispensations or privileges or tell him how to run his show (even if I'd do things some other way). I want to be there to fit in and be supportive of his effort and that of our other leaders at every level.

I hope I've learned that lesson—having had to run interference with so many people who have their own private agendas. They come at you constantly, and their motives are often not pure. They come to you because you're a figurehead in the Church, and they want something out of you for their own personal gain. Or they want to "make the Church over" according to their own particular preconceptions. They are takers and not givers.

Facing page, top row, left to right: Sister Wendy Bingham (Stepan) and young member child (courtesy Wendy Bingham Stepan), Sister Jenna Hughes (Tew) (Jenna Hughes Tew), and Elders Justin Stratton and Cory Wolfenbarger (Michael Hertig); *middle row:* Elder Jonathan Hart (Morgan Magleby), recently ordained, new-member father baptizing his daughter (Wendy Bingham Stepan), and Sister Jill Cherrington (Christensen) (Ray Banks); *bottom row:* young member feeding Elder Darrell Stubbs (Darrell Stubbs), and Elena Shkolyonok and Natasha Nepomnyashchaya.

Or they are dictators, the Church's secret rivals. They don't understand that—though we are a privileged part of Christ's Church—we do not own or control it. It is his Church, not ours. And as Elder C. Max Caldwell once pointed out to the mission presidencies assembled in Frankfurt, there is no one with a calling in the Church who is not accountable to someone else. Either we believe that, or our faith is deficient.

As a senior missionary, Bob Rees wrote us while serving as public relations representative in the Baltic Mission, "When you're working in a primary way with the basic issues of the gospel and with people who are learning them for the first time and employing them in their lives, there is no room or luxury for criticism or negativity. People who leave the Church have lost their memory of their primary witness from the Holy Ghost."

Aleksey and Anna Shcheglov and their children, *(left to right)* Veronika and Anastasiya. Aleksey was a counselor in a branch presidency.

Ties That Bind

I have had four major "chances" to draw my soul to the Lord—my mission in Germany in the fifties, my interaction with students in a BYU branch for two memorable years, my calling as a branch president at the Missionary Training Center for three more years (the best "ward" I ever lived in—assisting the spiritual hatching of fledgling missionaries), and most recently the term in St. Petersburg. These periods of more intense and utterly exhilarating Church service—ten and a half years in all—are perhaps a kind of tithing-in-time, in my case more than 10 percent in proportion to my years.

But how many chances does a fellow get? I really can't expect any more, so I had better make the most of this fourth one. As I wish for "my" (presumptuous adjective) missionaries, I also wish for myself that we will not forget what we have so recently seen and felt and to some extent been.

I recently redisplayed in my study here in Bountiful the pictures of our children in their younger years. It provoked a tremendous nostalgia and appreciation for what good people they've become and what marvelous potential they had back then (which I could not at the time so readily perceive). I wanted to cry—with gratitude and love and a feeling of utter unworthiness that I could claim them at all and now their children too. Then thoughts of the missionaries and members in Russia, with whom we can no longer so freely interact, evoked similar speculation. How are they and what will they do with their lives? And again my cup seemed very full.

People tend to become a little more cautious and unsure with age, which may be a saving grace for many of us. Elder Bruce D. Porter commented to our missionaries in St. Petersburg that, as he looks back at the diligently plodding as opposed to the zealous, effervescent Church types, the former seem in some cases to have held out better. Possibly he had persons such as me in mind (I was his former supervisor in the BYU Honors Program during his student days).

I would hope that for the rest of my life I would always, more so than before, make as a priority my family and any callings that come to me in the Church, that I would consider them to be very sacred and important and make time for them, not just have them be incidental to the other things I do. Although I will have other interests again, and they will compete, I know that I can and need to maintain the balance and gladly serve, gladly be there, as I'm expected to be, where the Church is concerned.

Sergey Smelov, president of the branch in Kolpino, a suburb of St. Petersburg, with his daughters Katya *(oldest)* and Diana.

I will probably find more time—make more time—to give greater quality attention to my family members, especially our fairly numerous grandchildren. Now that we've arrived at my ancestral home and the site of our eventual retirement, I often tell myself that I got here just in time. Our bishop and son-in-law, father of eight of our grandchildren, essentially called me to repentance in a letter we received shortly before our release:

> I was impressed with your comment (made on the phone the last time we spoke) about how during this mission you've come to a better understanding of what is really important in life. You mentioned you would be focusing more time and effort on being a grandfather and father and less on a number of your earlier pursuits.
>
> While both are worthy, I feel that many people could accomplish the latter, but only you will be able to be a loving, concerned, and

Elder Brian Tew and children in an orphanage

available grandfather to my children. You are their only living grandfather. You alone can function in that role, spend time with them, listen to them, hug them. I can do all these things as their father, but I cannot be their grandfather. To you alone has fallen the responsibility (and great blessing) to be our family patriarch. What you and Merriam do as grandparents will have a tremendous and lifelong effect on my children.

Kyra's due date is May 29, which means we will probably have this next baby by mid-June. This is the third baby she's carried while I've served in a bishopric. She's wrestled children in sacrament meeting on her own for almost four years. It is her most difficult trial, but she has done a wonderful job. As there are in missionary work, there may be challenges in "home life" after you return, but the end result will be immense joy and great satisfaction. We look forward to sharing all this with you upon your return.

Dima Zhuravlyov, called as a district mission leader at the age of sixteen.

Aleksandr and Yulya Tomak and their daughter, Natalya. As a relatively young member, Aleksandr served as president of St. Petersburg's largest district.

167

With my particular predilections, I have, unlike many another person, long believed that the greatest human achievements are neither technological (sports cars, airplanes) nor athletic (Olympic Golds or NFL/NBA wins). Instead I favor the great novels, the great symphonies, and memorable productions of profound plays, including certain rare films. I'm now prepared to add The Church of Jesus Christ of Latter-day Saints (in principle and practice) and families, as such. Each of these remarkable endeavors is polyphonic, dramatic, filled with tension, and subject to a spectrum of moods and sensations. All of them challenge, stretch, sensitize, enlighten, edify, and enhance the individual.

Conduit

I'm a strong believer that the Lord operates mostly through people. Therefore I put a lot of stock in what the spiritual example of another reveals about the gospel and things sacred. Such inspiration doesn't come just from

Sister Valeriya (last name unknown), Dmitry Nikitin (former branch president and current mission building specialist), and Sister Wendy Bingham (Stepan).

leaders. It also comes in the person of your average member, from his or her timid faithfulness.

Because we are the Lord's instruments, other people are or should be the focus of our aspirations, our personal attention. In our quest to see God's face, what most matters in mortality is how we face one another—with what patience, tenderness, mercy, and good humor. As we caringly view and treat each other, we sense the love and beauty of his countenance.

How do the Church and its teachings help us draw near to him as we face one another? Much as I resist formulas, another has recently occurred to me. It's a sort of dialectic that sums up as much as anything what I am grateful to believe about the gospel and the Church, its necessary vehicle:

Courtesy Morgan Magleby

President Viktor Yakovlev, first counselor in the mission presidency.

1. Everyone wishes to be happy.
2. Happiness is ultimately predicated on the capacity to love others—even more than it is on being loved, which is its inevitable reciprocal.
3. We can love only those we authentically get to know.
4. We know one another authentically only as we interact in other than superficial ways, particularly as we serve each other.
5. The service this requires cannot be just of our choosing but requires sacrifice, the kind we would otherwise tend to avoid. That kind of sacrifice is predicated upon works, chief of which involves our ongoing individual need for repentance. This requires a willingness to act upon what we need to do rather than simply what we want to do. The Church is better than anything else I know of at requiring such a response from us.
6. We can endure in the mode of sacrifice only if we allow the Spirit to sustain us. An especially important aspect of living with the Spirit is to remain genuinely, sensitively engaged in one another's lives, to give unconditional attention to others. In so doing, each of us will continue to be a conduit for the Light of the World.

Vyacheslav and Evgeniya Alimpiev with President and Sister Rogers. Vyacheslav was president of the first Kaliningrad Branch.

Discoveries of a Mission: Things Witnessed, Experienced, and Hopefully Learned

This is the list I come up with when people ask, "What special insights came to you during your mission—what principles did you see in operation to a degree you did not before?" The missionary experience fully validates each of the following and many another of the restored gospel's truth claims. If it could not do this, many missionaries and convert members would not emerge from that experience so positively engaged and profoundly transformed.

1. The transforming power that comes with accepting a call and serving in the two-year-long "boot camp" we call a mission. This immediate blessing comes only by doing the hardest thing the missionaries have done thus far. As one of the missionaries so poignantly reminded me,

   > I often feel alone. I want to feel a part of this effort and would hope people would stop assuming that I'm just here kicking against the pricks and try to understand where I am really

"coming from." If you have any suggestions about how I can approach life differently, I'd appreciate them. I also hope I have cast off any concerns about rebelliousness or immaturity in my dealings with you. Since you have described perfection as an ongoing process, let's try and appreciate this 20-year-old kid's as an effort to move forward.

The arduous effort a mission requires not only spiritualizes and disciplines but also renders its participants far more fit to succeed in all areas of life—school, marriage, profession.

2. The palpable engagement of the Spirit, which enriches and radically changes the lives of many—missionaries, investigators, and members—for the better. Like no other association I can comprehend, the Church affords us a wonderful spectrum of acquaintances we would never otherwise get to know, including many whose lives are noticeably transformed by the Spirit. Through the Spirit's influence, our interaction "opens" others' lives to us and ours to them. This would not happen if we were allowed to "pick and choose" those we might care to worship with or minister to.

Courtesy Morgan Magleby

Elder Morgan Magleby, replacing a "saturated" water filter.

In the mission field, relationships with others are neither militant, smug, complacent, nor insipid. We soon learn that our faith increases as we testify and that our charity enlarges as we extend ourselves toward others. We then feel the Spirit's undeniable presence. We learn that, by so asserting ourselves, we are even more blessed than our hearers or the recipients of our concern and care. I'm eager for my grandchildren to serve missions and see the Church at its most viable and best.

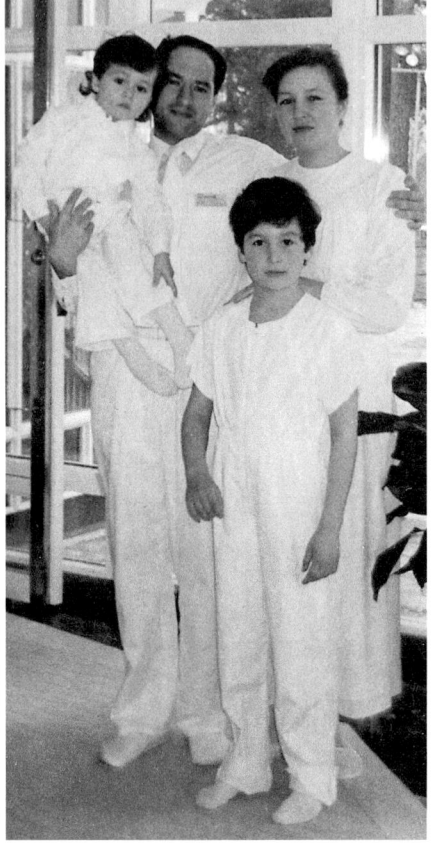

3. The strength and stature that derive from surrendering ourselves to higher powers. Paradoxically, our distinct, authentic selves and our true nobility most fully emerge when we surrender our self-interest and, in concert with others, freely submit to divine will.

   Although the Lord's servants at all levels are extended inordinate trust and accountability for others' salvation and their own, the truly dedicated recognize that they and the things they try to accomplish with their own effort are literally nothing. Solutions come about despite their efforts and from a source far beyond their capabilities or sphere of influence. For instance, Elder Dennis B. Neuenschwander has pointed out that "no one knows better than the Brethren that the rules for missionaries are not just from them [the Brethren]." A further instance: over and over again, when the right leader was needed in a branch or district in the St. Petersburg area, he or she was invariably raised up, even when the pool for such was terribly thin. Miraculously, there appeared a man- or woman-of-the-hour.

4. The role of the gospel and the Church in combating serious social ills—alcoholism and other forms of addiction, disintegration of families and consequent neglect and abuse of children, etc. Everything we do in the Church is sacred because it is directed at preserving and enhancing the quality of life itself in all its forms. This lofty purpose manifests itself in such practical areas as sustaining health and in such motivating perspectives as the Church's emphasis on enduring marriage and family relations.

   I like to testify not only to the truthfulness of the Church but also to its importance in our lives. Clearly, importance follows truthfulness but needs to be affirmed as well.

5. The motivating power of the cosmic doctrine of literal divine "sonship" and the promise of eternal family relationships. Our heightened sense of kinship with Deity enhances our appreciation for our own family with the realization that we are eternally "theirs" and they eternally "ours," just as we are all "his," or at least can be.

Top left: Young Russian girl in autumn attire.

Top right: Anatoly and Irina Sitonin and their children, *(left to right)* Nikita and Vitaly.

Left: Andrey and Larisa Slepukhin *(far right)* and their children, *(left to right)* Daniil, Aleksandra, Anna *(baby)*, and Evgeniya.

6. Spiritual camouflage—the unfathomability to men's minds of sacred truth. During their ministries, both the Savior and Joseph Smith were rejected by most of their contemporaries. They were viewed as strange, threatening, and false to those with only normal powers of reason and comprehension (the "natural men"). Similarly, what for others (and sometimes ourselves) seems utterly unnatural must needs include

   - whatever pertains to the transcendent nature of the Restoration
   - what impels missionaries to speak to others
   - whatever at times motivates us to serve others sacrificially, to love and forgive enemies, and to wish their forgiveness, to bless those who despitefully use us. Our genocide-obsessed world cannot begin to grasp, but desperately needs, this vision.
   - what motivates people to subdue their physical appetites and live by the Word of Wisdom and the law of chastity
   - what so unexpectedly causes a teenage Russian boy in a land steeped in racial prejudice to ask a black African student member to baptize him. (Flying back from that baptism in Kaliningrad, we felt we had somehow experienced a piece of heaven.)

   By the same token, those who lack a witness of our message cannot possibly appreciate or value it. Nor should we expect them to. It can only seem both bizarre to them as well as untrue. We can communicate about it only on a level other than that of rational discourse. This camouflage protects what is sacred from those not prepared to accept it.

7. The sad recognition that, "while many want the Church to help them change the world, few want to help the Church change the world" (Dr. Talmage Neilson). This truth applies as much to members with impure, self-serving motives as it does to outsiders.

8. Anticipating one's departure home and release, one senses, a real personal emptiness and loss—a kind of minideath. Yet how analogous this is to other stages in one's life. And how compensatory that we could then return to our seven children and eighteen living grandchildren (now twenty-five), seven of them born during our three years in Russia. (So why should we fear death—a further, beautiful commencement in expanding and intensifying relationships with others?)

Affirmation

The work in which we are called to serve, the great blessing it affords every human being on an eternal scale if he or she will only respond to it, is certainly the work of the Lord. And that blessing is, from my perspective, accessible in its fullness only through the one Church with which the Lord is well pleased, The Church of Jesus Christ of Latter-day Saints.

It is a further witness that in the seemingly alien environment and culture of Russia, there were still those who heard our missionaries' message and now feel the Spirit so deeply. The genuineness of their conversion is evidenced by their remarkable faith, humility, enthusiasm, and eagerness to serve. Even those who were our branch presidents for a time and are no longer with us once manifested those same qualities and clearly felt the Spirit. They have just forgotten it and not allowed it to continue as a force that pulsates in them and informs their lives. The Spirit is that tenuous.

I say this in the name of Jesus Christ. Amen.

Andrey Lermontov and President Rogers

Afterword

Gary Anderson, President of the
Russia St. Petersburg Mission, 1996–1998

"What was your mission like?" The answer is hard to articulate but usually goes something like this: "It was one of the most difficult things I have done, but also one of the most enjoyable. It is like the ocean waves crashing on the shore—they keep coming at you, and sometimes they are a lot higher than at other times."

As we departed for St. Petersburg, we wondered how long we would even be there. General Aleksandr Lebed had just made his caustic and very derogatory comments about Mormons in Russia, and the news media were speculating that missionaries would soon be expelled from the country. This attitude was not shared by any Church leaders who talked to us, but as we flew into the airport, there was some trepidation and a feeling that we were not exactly welcome. This perception was heightened to some extent as we stepped off the airplane and were greeted by the sight of fully uniformed soldiers with AK-47s hanging from their shoulders. Our concerns eased somewhat as we were greeted by President and Sister Rogers and the assistants and by the discovery that only one piece of our family's luggage had been lost. The airline representatives assured us that it would soon be located and delivered right to our door.

After spending a few short hours with the Rogerses, we were on our own. The waves started crashing on the shore and did not abate until the handoff to President and Sister Roland Datwyler occurred at the end of our mission. Something quite interesting did happen. I started to understand why I was there, and I was prompted to formulate some objectives to be accomplished. Fundamentally, it was time to establish a firm foundation upon which a stake could be established. This task would encompass not only the human side of the equation but the physical facilities side as well.

My background as an attorney for over twenty years has been to work with businesses and individuals in structuring appropriate legal entities and frameworks for successful operation. I have represented real estate firms, title companies, construction companies, and architectural firms. I have tried to help clients understand that it is much easier and less expensive to avoid problems than it is to get out of them once they are in. In addition, I have had extensive experience working with boards of both for-profit and not-for-profit entities. I have learned much about conflict resolution and ways to work through major problems and broker solutions. It is in this context that I recognized a significant need in the Russia St. Petersburg Mission—to find places for the members to meet and come together for baptisms, meetings, activities, and worship.

At the time of our arrival, the physical facility situation had one bright star in an otherwise bleak universe. The first and only chapel in Russia had been completed in Vyborg, approximately three hours' travel time from St. Petersburg. Otherwise, there was one permanent rental in a city of five million people. Permanent rental was defined as a facility that could be utilized on a day other than Sunday and was therefore not used by someone else. All the other rentals were Sunday-only and were used by schools, businesses, and libraries or as wedding chapels during the week.

There were approximately twenty branches in St. Petersburg and several others in smaller cities in the surrounding region as well as in Kaliningrad. Our baptisms took place in *banyas,* and every Sunday was an adventure. Besides having to bring all of the materials to be used each Sunday, we faced other challenges. It was quite possible that because of an election or a holiday we would be told a few days in advance that a facility would not be available for Sunday. The heating situation was unpredictable, and sometimes meetings would have to be shortened because even coats and hats were not sufficient protection against the cold. The need for better facilities seemed to be an area where my background and talents could be utilized.

The second need was to continue the excellent work of President Rogers in shifting more and more leadership responsibility to the local members. Almost every day, I gave thanks for the obvious contribution he had made in training leaders—both men and women—and empowering them to lead their own fellow members. Given my experience in Church leadership and in secular pursuits, I could see opportunities to involve the Russian members in resolving problems and in helping others actualize their potential. One observation I made after a while was that, as oppressive and disastrous as the Communist Party had been for the citizenry in general, many of our most skilled leaders came from Party backgrounds. Universal leadership principles seemed to surface even in the Party.

Based on some of these perceptions, I was formulating in my mind a general plan of attack for my service in the mission when I received a telephone call from Elder Dennis B. Neuenschwander of the Area Presidency, who was completing his service in the Europe East Area and was returning to Salt Lake City for another assignment. He called to wish us well and asked me whether I had received any particular impressions in the six weeks I had been on the job. I told him that I had, and he said I should write them down so they would be a guide for me. He said it had been his experience that whenever he was called to a new assignment, the Lord blessed him with particular insight at the outset that, if written down and reviewed often,

Courtesy Gary and Sheryl Anderson

Gary and Sheryl Anderson

would give him direction for the entire assignment. He said that if this were ignored it would tend to get lost in the daily battle later on. I followed his advice and concur with his observations.

With this as background, let me touch on a few points that can perhaps update and give continuity to some of the threads which Tom Rogers has so eloquently woven. I recognized early on that I would not be able to attempt to follow all the tracks which a person such as he had made. His lifetime of study and teaching about Russian language and culture was a tough act to follow when it came to things Russian, especially in a literary context. Fortunately, the members seemed to understand that I brought a different set of talents and abilities and weaknesses, and they were consequently very accepting. However, there were times I sensed some frustration when they tried to overcome communication barriers. Also, there is a very human tendency to discount others' talents when some weaknesses, such as language, are so very obvious.

For me, the benefit of my weaknesses was a daily dose of humiliation, which I hope was translated into humility. I learned in a way difficult to express that what Moses termed the "nothingness of man" is literally true

(Moses 1:10). I learned that without God's help it would be impossible even to survive from day to day. But with perseverance and his help, great things would come to pass.

One theme which recurred until the end of my mission was the uncertainty of the Church's status in Russia. What started with Lebed just before we arrived continued. Our wonderful nonmember attorney, Dmitry Silchenkov, called me a couple of months after our arrival to advise me of a meeting called by the head of the St. Petersburg Committee on Religious Affairs. The purpose of the meeting was to receive comments on the draft legislation proposed in the local legislative body to severely restrict the activities of religious groups. We attended the meeting along with a number of other religious leaders and expressed our concerns in a written response to the legislation. The lady who headed the committee had quite an enlightened view of religious freedom. However, she was dealing with factions from other religious and atheistic groups that would dearly love to limit proselytizing and other forms of religious activity. A law that was quite restrictive was ultimately passed, but fortunately the governor of St. Petersburg vetoed the bill on constitutional grounds.

This veto gave only brief respite until another crisis loomed on the federal level: we got wind of a very restrictive bill being proposed in the Duma in Moscow that would impact the whole country. This bill, which was heavily publicized in the Western press, was adopted by the Duma, vetoed by President Yeltsin, but ultimately enacted into law with some significant changes. Some of its most oppressive elements were eliminated, but until May 1998, when the Church's new charter was approved, the impact on the Church's activities was potentially very damaging.

In connection with this law and pressures from other segments of society, problems were ever present. There were new restrictions on visas. There were questions about the tax status of the Church's organizations and the missionaries. There were pressures from the local police concerning tracting, contacting, and setting up street displays. There were unwritten or private directives to local schools, supposedly about the separation of church and state facilities, which resulted in the termination of our rental arrangements with schools. In some schools, restrictions were placed on missionaries who were giving service in the form of teaching English or coaching sports. The case alluded to by Tom Rogers in his piece about the thugs who broke into a meeting and physically abused some missionaries finally came to trial (see "Shocker," p. 91). Its only television coverage broadcast the testimony of one of the thugs making libelous statements about the Church in an attempt to justify his actions. Ultimately, the thugs were convicted of a minor crime but were not punished in any significant way.

Another negative impact was on the expansion of the Church. Our mission as well as the others in Russia had designated cities that we felt should be opened to missionary work, even if we had to do it without adding to our missionary force. Because of the uncertainty caused by the new law, no expansion could be authorized. A few months after our arrival—before this law was passed—we had opened Petrozavodsk, the capitol of the Republic of Karelia, which runs adjacent to the border of Finland. This was done under the existing law and in accordance with the Church's charter, and from a legal and ecclesiastical standpoint, it went very smoothly. For our 1997 plan, we had slated several other cities for missionary work, but all that was stymied, and the only new areas that were opened were within the Leningrad Province, where the Church was already registered.

After much behind-the-scenes work and the very welcome assistance of United States and European government leaders and religious freedom advocates, the Church was granted a very favorable charter in May 1998, giving us the authority to operate a full scope of Church programs and missionary work. While I recognize that the battle still has not been conclusively won, as I analyze the Church's standing in Russia compared to where it was when I arrived, I note significant progress.

My own sense is that the Lord has used past forms of opposition to his own advantage. The comments by Lebed gave much recognition to the Mormons, and people became curious about this group of people that were supposedly so dastardly. When they met missionaries who belied the negative images, they were interested in hearing more. When President Clinton took up the cause with Prime Minister Chernomyrdin, the Church gained some validity. When Senators Bennett, Hatch, and Smith made trips to Russia on behalf of freedom for all religions, it was well known that they were Mormons. Much good publicity came from a piece that was broadcast on Channel 1, the most widely watched TV station in the country. In a program called *The Travel Club*, which is known to virtually every Russian, the reenactment in Russia of the pioneers' trek along the Mormon Trail was shown in a very favorable light, and people connected it with the Church in Russia.

It is obvious from the assurances given the Church by high Russian government officials and the ultimate approval of the Church's charter that The Church of Jesus Christ of Latter-day Saints is becoming better known and respected. Even though this recognition is somewhat grudgingly given in certain quarters. At the very least there is an understanding that the Church is not to be dismissed lightly. In fact, my thought is there is a general feeling that there are easier targets to shoot at than the Mormons. This may take us out of the line of fire in the future.

One experience may illustrate at least one positive perception. Since the mission home and office are in such close proximity to the Hermitage and most visitors want to visit it, I became interested in an advertisement that appeared in the St. Petersburg *Times*. The advertisement announced the establishment of a new club called Friends of the Hermitage, similar to the support groups for most cultural institutions in the United States. For a set yearly fee, I learned I could join this club and have free entry any time to the Hermitage. I decided to join and became a charter member.

In the course of this association, I discussed with the club's staff whether there were any kinds of service opportunities for our missionaries (having in mind such mundane tasks as hauling crates or cleaning). They told me they would think about it and get back to me. A few days later, I received a call from a certain Svetlana, who told me she would like to talk about our offer. I made an appointment and met with her and her boss, who asked whether our missionaries would be willing to assist them at the front counter of the museum. They were to explain the benefits of the friends club to foreign visitors and help them fill out the paperwork, as well as work with the Russian-speaking cashiers to recruit for the club. Ultimately, these arrangements were made, and missionary companionships have been using their weekly service time to work in this capacity.

The point I want to make, however, is related to a conversation I had when we were navigating the relationship between this world-class museum and the fact that these young men and women were LDS missionaries. In our discussion, I posed the question about what should happen if museum patrons or staff were to ask why the volunteers are in Russia and why they have learned to speak Russian. The museum's response was that our volunteers should feel free to explain that they are missionaries and that they are doing service. The museum knew that people would be curious, and they were just pleased that the missionaries were willing to help the museum. I was given to understand that these issues had been discussed with the museum's administration.

The response to my second question was even more interesting. I asked whether they were concerned that other churches, including the Russian Orthodox Church, might object to our involvement with the Hermitage, a great national institution. They said they did not care if other churches objected or not. After all, they were not volunteering their people, were they?

Back to the need for places to meet: it was in this context that some of the conventional wisdom simply did not apply to our situation. Logically, there is a protocol that is supposed to be followed in acquiring meeting facilities. When a branch is first established, we try to locate Sunday-only premises. This works in the beginning and is certainly adequate for a start-up branch. However, as numbers increase, it is important to move to more permanent accommodations.

We had assumed that the next step would be to rent facilities that could be utilized throughout the week as well as on Sunday. Unfortunately, that option was not generally available. Another consideration was that rental rates were so high that in many cases the rent would be sufficient to amortize the cost to purchase a facility within three to five years. Since the transition into a free-market economy is still in process, real estate being no exception, there were numerous hurdles that needed to be overcome, many of which were not well understood by the various Church committees that had to approve such acquisitions.

Perhaps because of my background and also because the Church had been in St. Petersburg longer than any other place in Russia, our mission became a focus for efforts to find adequate facilities for the Saints. The set of talents and experience I had seemed to fit this task. Our local attorney and I were able to work closely together, not only to acquire facilities for our mission, but also to help bring about changes in the system so that progress could be made in the future to accomplish this goal.

We soon learned that the lack of appropriate facilities was a significant obstacle in establishing a stake. For those members who are accustomed to driving to the next corner for Sunday meetings, being able to go to the meetinghouse library for prepared packets of teaching materials, meeting in comfortable rooms with nice chairs and tolerable temperatures, and attending baptisms in conducive surroundings (the list could go on and on), it is hard to understand what our Russian members were contending with. Besides the effort to travel on public transport at significant expense for up to an hour, the location and circumstances once they arrived could be enough to discourage further attendance. If it was bad for members, it was worse for investigators. In any event, three new properties were acquired before our departure, and ten more had been approved (although not all of them may come to fruition). The fact that this particular need was something that I felt very competent and comfortable to address was further assurance that God knows what is going on in a micro as well as a universal sense.

Another obstacle to the establishment of a stake is common everywhere—lack of priesthood leadership. While the mission had over two thousand members, we still did not have sufficient, seasoned leadership to conduct Church affairs without assistance from the mission office, the mission president, and the missionaries. After all, many of the leaders had been members for only three to five years, and very few over seven.

It was, again, in this area that my experience in working with Church councils and with a number of boards proved invaluable. Because of the strong organization I inherited from Tom Rogers, significant strides could be made in shifting more responsibility to the local leaders. One of my counselors was a Russian, and after Elder Gail Halvorsen's departure, a second Russian counselor was called. Both were able to hold interviews and were given direct responsibility for mission districts, as well as specific assignments such as the youth programs or the temple. We were also able to replace missionaries serving as branch presidents with Russian members so that only the newest branches were presided over by missionaries.

Through all of this growth, I clearly came to understand that many experiences in my previous life were indispensable in helping move this maturation process along. After a particularly energetic meeting in which strong positions had been expressed in a very active fashion, I asked one of my counselors whether this type of meeting was normal. He just smiled and said, "Whenever you get three Russians together, you will have at least four opinions." Over time, the meetings seemed to operate more smoothly, and I eventually grew to admire many of these leaders, both men and women, because of their extraordinary leadership capacity. Many times what they lacked in experience was made up for with love and wisdom.

During our stay, the last of the standard Church handbooks was translated and published in Russian. In our final year, virtually every manual and handbook which was available to members in English was also available in Russian. This fact was not lost on the Russian members. January 1998 marked a very important time in the Church's history in Russia because at that time Russia became a Phase Three country, meaning that the curriculum available in the heartland of the Church was also available and being taught in the branches of the mission. The manual which is being used in priesthood and Relief Society lessons, *The Teachings of the Prophets: Brigham Young,* marked a significant milestone. Several members came to me with tears in their eyes and asked me to thank whoever was responsible for making that book and its teachings available to them in their native tongue. When all this happened, I sensed a higher level of commitment and confidence from the members.

Another very interesting aspect of the experience was the marvelous opportunity to work with a number of missionaries who came from Russian and former Soviet-bloc countries. Along with the first missionaries from cities like Omsk, Perm, and Engels, there were missionaries from Moscow, Rostov, and Samara. Other countries represented included Ukraine, Armenia, Moldavia, Hungary, East Germany, the Czech Republic, Poland, Mongolia, and Belorussia.

Since these missionaries did not have the opportunity to attend a Missionary Training Center unless they spoke English, they came without that training and without going through the temple. In a few cases, they came with no prior knowledge of Russian. Sometimes, when they had difficulties adjusting, I reminded the other missionaries that very often their non-American counterparts had had little Church experience. Many had been members for only one or two years and did not have even the basic preparation for missions or language training imparted in the MTC. I tried to teach the concept that going an extra mile for these missionaries was helping to establish the foundation of the Church in their countries upon their return home.

In several cases, these non-Americans were among the most outstanding of all our missionaries. Every effort to help them be successful was repaid tenfold. I truly believe they will be every bit as important to the growth of the Church in their native countries as the first generation pioneers were in Utah. I was often very humbled by their tremendous faith and dedication. My hope is that they will return and marry in the temple and raise a righteous generation of Church members.

This cross-cultural experience has been on-going in the Church for many years as Wasatch Front Mormons serve missions across the globe. However, it has a particular impact on Church members who are trying to deal with not-so-distant history. Several missionaries from former Soviet-bloc countries told me that their family members were not thrilled that their son or daughter was going to Russia to serve a mission. After all, the animosity against Russia since the fall of the Iron Curtain is quite strong.

But the love that transcends boundaries was never more apparent than the first visit to Russia by Elder F. Enzio Busche. He is, of course, a German who grew up during the Second World War. The attitude of Russians toward Nazis in St. Petersburg, which lost fully half of its population during the 900-day siege, is very bitter. Given that backdrop, Elder Busche was understandably apprehensive as he attended a district conference on that first visit to Russia. However, as the meeting progressed, he shared his own personal struggles during the war and talked about the fact that he had been reading Tolstoy's book entitled *Resurrection* when the missionaries contacted him. Tolstoy's writing had sensitized him to their message. At that juncture in his address, it became apparent that a bond had formed between him and the Russian congregation. The Russian members could relate to his suffering on a human level, and they responded to his knowledge of one of their beloved authors. Afterward, there was an outpouring of genuine love that removed Elder Busche's concerns and left him deeply moved, and he clearly reciprocated that love.

One marvelous blessing was the association with members of the Area Presidency as well as with other visitors from Church headquarters. They are truly committed and dedicated servants of the Lord. Their area covers thirty-five countries and stretches from North Africa to the middle of

Siberia. The cultures and languages could not be more diverse and difficult, but despite these challenges, they always bring with them an energy and optimism that are sorely needed. That outlook is even more remarkable when one realizes that they routinely deal with the difficult problems we are either unable or unauthorized to handle. In all their activities, these Brethren seldom get the opportunity to experience the personal contact that brought me so much joy.

Any discussion of that joy is not complete without mentioning the really rewarding experience of working with very high-caliber missionaries, including four senior missionary couples, most of whom were from the United States. The missionaries we received were usually quite extraordinary. Their innocence and faith was contagious, not only to us but also to the members and investigators. Perhaps part of their effectiveness is attributable to the fact that they did not know any better, but many times I was in awe of their sheer indomitable spirit. In a spiritual sense, I felt as though I were in the presence of giants.

Challenges will continue and will also change as they changed after the Rogerses left. The economic situation continues to be problematic. Even though there is on-going construction in St. Petersburg, the fundamentals of a stable economic system are still not firmly in place. One huge frustration for all Russians is the Western influence flooding into their country. Culturally, this influx is a problem. The level of pornography and other adverse phenomena is appalling. More than one Russian has commented on the fact that, after *glasnost,* the Russian media got plugged into the sewers of the West.

Another tragedy is the flood of alcohol, tobacco, and drugs that has helped reduce the life expectancy of the Russian male to fifty-six years. (It is obvious that the pressures brought to bear on American and European cigarette companies in the United States and Europe have caused a commercial exodus to other less paternalistic countries. This onslaught threatens to deprive countries such as Russia of a healthy rising generation.) Images of miniskirted girls wearing Pall Mall t-shirts passing out cigarettes indiscriminately on the streets of St. Petersburg are over-shadowed only by memories of teenage boys on the streets at nine or ten o'clock in the morning in an obviously intoxicated state. Certainly, these problems stem partly from Russia's own past, but the advertising and distribution methods are Western in origin. It was ironic that the only recognizable pictures of Utah that I saw on Russian billboards were the red-rock scenes of Monument Valley that served as a backdrop for the Marlboro man.

There is no doubt in my mind that God's plan is moving forward on the earth. When Elder Jeffrey R. Holland visited our mission in fall 1997, he said something I have reflected on many times since. He said that the older he gets the less certain he is about most things, but the more certain he is about one thing—that God's kingdom will continue to grow until it fills the whole earth as prophesied by Daniel. His only concern is whether he will be part of it. I am convinced that God's kingdom will continue to move forward on the earth, including Russia, and that everything the prophets have foretold will indeed come to pass. My mission experience has helped me to see this more clearly and has also aided me in my endeavors to be part of that kingdom when it really counts.

My final thoughts are of gratitude—gratitude for the experience; gratitude for predecessors like the Rogerses; gratitude for missionaries before, during, and after our stewardship; gratitude for members who have imparted more to me than I have given to them and more than I can express; gratitude for Church leaders who had confidence enough to issue the call and dedication enough to sustain me in the call; gratitude for a wife and children who were there and know what it was like and lived through this experience with me; and gratitude for God's mercy and love. It was a marvelous adventure.

Name Index

Page numbers for photographs are in **boldface.**

187

Topic Index

About the Author

A former director of the BYU Honors Program, Thomas F. Rogers is a professor of Russian language and literature at Brigham Young University. He has traveled extensively in Russia, Eastern Europe, and India. He and his wife, Merriam, were called as missionaries in 1993 to Russia, where Rogers presided over the Russia St. Petersburg Mission for three years.

Author of more than a dozen plays, many on Mormon subjects, he studied at the Yale School of Drama and holds degrees from the University of Utah, Yale, and Georgetown. He has also studied theater in Poland and Russian at Moscow State University and taught at Howard University in Washington, D.C., and at the University of Utah. In 1998 he received the Mormon Festival of the Arts lifetime service award for his contribution to LDS theater and dramaturgy.

The Rogerses are the parents of seven children and reside in Bountiful, Utah.